MORE
BIRMINGHAM
MEMORIES

The publishers would like to thank the following companies for their

support in the production of this book

Alcoa Europe Flat Rolled Products
Alwayse Engineering Limited
Armac Brassworks
BID - Services with Deaf People
Birmingham College of Food, Tourism and Creative Studies
Cookes Furniture Ltd
Darlingtons Travel Service
Doorfit Products
Louis Drapkin Ltd
Durolas (Contractors) Ltd
Edgbaston High School for Girls
Fircroft College
F.G.F. Ltd
A J Gilbert (Birmingham) Ltd
Samuel Groves & Co. Limited
S Lilley & Son
Lodge Tyre Co. Ltd
Midland Welding Supply Company
Rainsord And Lynes Limited/ Bullfinch (Gas Equipment) Limited
Salts Healthcare Ltd
Savekers Group
Scrivens Optical And Hearing Care
Silk & Terry Ltd
Smiths Aerospace Components - Tyseley Ltd
E H Smith Group of Companies
E W Tinegate Ltd
Welconstruct Group
Whites Removals & Transport Ltd
W Wing Yip Plc

First published in Great Britain by True North Books Limited
England HX3 6AE
01422 344344

ISBN 1 903204 80 1

Text, design and origination by True North Books Limited
Printed and bound by The Amadeus Press Limited

MORE
BIRMINGHAM
MEMORIES

Contents

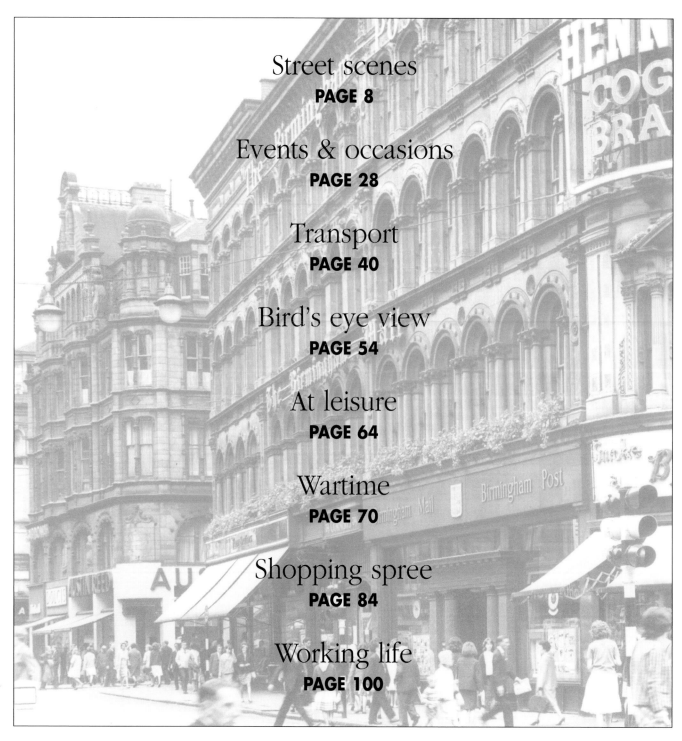

Introduction

Every so often we get the opportunity to indulge ourselves in a little nostalgia. Where is the harm in that? As human beings we just love to hark back to the past and relive some of the good times, but also ponder on the lessons we have learned from mistakes made or the less enjoyable moments of recent history. Our lives have been particularly affected by the way our society has developed over the last century. Going back to when grandma was just a young woman, motor cars were something of a rarity on the driveway, electricity was still a novelty, the radio a new form of entertainment and aeroplanes seemed to be held together by bits of wire and strong glue. She used the outdoor lavvy, not the flushing toilet upstairs, and took her bath in an old tub dragged in from the back yard and filled by kettles heated on an open range. Our grandparents, though, had a sense of family and togetherness that they would not have exchanged for all of your modern conveniences. There was a bonding and community spirit that today's rapid way of life and wider horizons seems to have lost as relatives have scattered across

the country and to outposts on the other side of the globe. Even when our parents were young and travel became easier, domestic appliances more affordable and a greater variety of entertainment on offer, their lifestyle was at some distance from the way we conduct ourselves in the 21st century. Many of the changes are for the good. Poverty is no longer a major blight and the advances in medical science have seen our life expectancy rise dramatically as the last century unfolded.

To complement these personal social changes, our surroundings have altered dramatically as well. 'More Birmingham Memories' provides readers with the opportunity to consider these and to make up their own mind as to the benefits, or otherwise, of such a metamorphosis. Our buildings, dress sense and working patterns have altered, partly from circumstance and sometimes by design. Within these pages the reader will be able to observe the differences in and around our city as we move through the middle years of the last century. For the more mature of us, there will be scenes that we recall at first hand, whereas younger people can take the opportunity to

enjoy a glimpse of how our city functioned before they were born. They will also be able to see streets, shops and events that their parents told them about, brought to life by the wonder of the images contained in this book. Each photograph is accompanied by text that is only intended in part to be informative. Its other purpose is to provoke discussion and, perhaps, controversial recollection amongst readers of just what it was like to be living through the times that are focused upon. Sometimes our memories can play tricks and things really were not quite as we think they used to be. At least the camera does not lie, though individual interpretation of what we can see may be more debatable. Whatever the result, there is little doubt that 'More Birmingham Memories' will stir a few nostalgic thoughts and startle one or two people whose recall is not quite as accurate as they might have led us to believe.

This book is not meant to be a dry and dusty tome, concentrating on the history of Birmingham as seen from the perspective of a textbook. Even so, it is pertinent to consider some elements of the far and distant past that have helped shape the modern city and its inhabitants. As with most of England, some small evidence of Bronze Age settlement can be found and the influence of the Roman occupation observed. However, it was in the Saxon era that the first true hamlet was found here. In the 6th and 7th centuries it was home to the tribe that made its home within the thickly forested area, initially under the leadership of a chief called Boerma. It is not too far a leap to link his name with that of the modern city, being the home or 'ham' of that tribe or 'ing' led by this particular Saxon. Some of the modern local place names provide further signs of a connection with these times. The suffix 'ley' means 'forest', so Moseley, Warley and Yardley, among others, were, in all probability, originally small settlements in clearings in the mighty forest. William the Conqueror established a survey of his new kingdom after he arrived on our shores in 1066. By 1086, the Domesday Book was completed as the most remarkable administrative accomplishment of the Middle Ages. Peter de Birmingham was named as the lord of the manor, though the population in the immediate area was insignificant and his lands were valued at a modest 20 shillings. Aston was the largest settlement, but even that could only boast 43 adults living there. When the right to hold a weekly market was granted by Henry II in 1156, the foundations were laid for the growth in importance of what was eventually to become Britain's second city. Cloth making and trading, one of Birmingham's first true industries,

was a major feature of the rise in prosperity that helped it become the third largest town in Warwickshire by the middle of the 14th century. The 17th century English Civil War provided an opportunity for industrial diversification. The manufacture of metal goods, especially swords, pikes and armour, enhanced the town's reputation as an industrial and commercial centre.

By the time that the first influences of the industrial revolution came to the midlands, Birmingham had, for the late 18th century, a large population of nearly 25,000. Birmingham imported the raw material for its already established iron trade that included the manufacture of toys, guns and buttons. Influential intellectuals formed the Lunar Society and brought together scientists and engineers to discuss their ideas and inventions. Boulton, Watt, Priestley and Wedgewood were just some of the major names involved. By the start of the 19th century, particularly under the influence of James Watt, it was literally a case of full steam ahead. Canals and the later railways improved connections with the outside world and, by the 1850s, Birmingham was established as the being the heartland of British industry. By now, the population was well into six figures and, under the inspired guidance of social reformer Joseph Chamberlain, the architectural face of domestic and municipal Birmingham radically changed. City status was granted in 1889 and it moved into the 20th century with an international reputation.

We are now ready to turn the pages on the 20th century, but with a concentration on those days from the interwar years to the start of the 70s. In fashion terms, it will be a journey from flappers to flares. For motorists, we will move from the Riley to the Range Rover and, for musicians, from Basie to Black Sabbath. On this nostalgic voyage, brought to you by courtesy of 'More Birmingham Memories', we will notice how language and attitudes evolve. Junk and grass were once rubbish and something to mow, not social evils as they became. Women were only too pleased to become housewives and the kitchen sink was a place to do the washing up, not some form of gloomy 1950s' drama. Girls once went out for the evening in pretty frocks, not crop tops revealing lumps of metal injected into the middle of their stomachs, and boys gallantly escorted them home, hoping for a peck on the cheek and not something far too basic to describe here. It is time to open a bottle of M & B's Deer's Leap and raise a glass to this trip down memory lane.

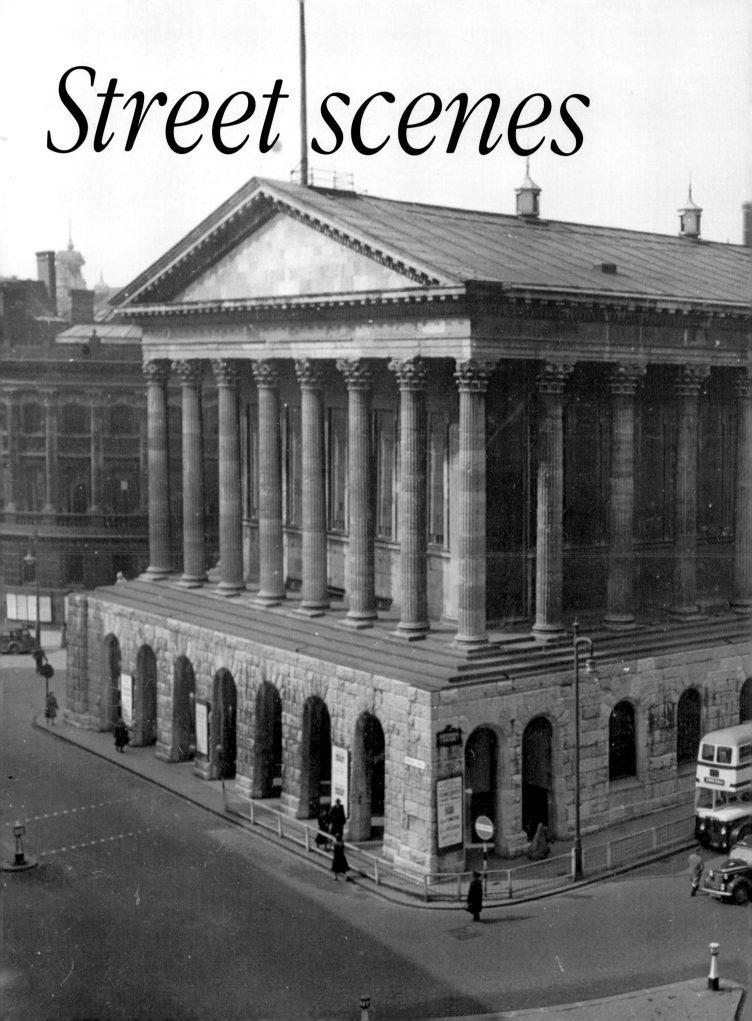

Street scenes

The cameraman stood on top of the old Post Office buildings to take this 1950s' photograph of the Town Hall. The cabs that Joseph Hansom patented in 1834 no longer drive past here, but the magnificent building that he helped design still stands as a tribute to the genius, vision and craftsmanship of people who took a true pride in their work. Hansom's building opened in the year that his low, two-wheeled, closed carriage was patented. Its distinctive features of the elevated driver's seat in the rear and passenger entrance from the front, through a folding door that gave access to the two person seat above the axle, would have been impressive as 19th century gentry bowled along. The driver spoke to the passengers through a trapdoor on top, but generally kept his counsel. The site for the Town Hall was purchased in 1830 and a competition held from which the most impressive design was chosen. The winning duo of Hansom and Welch were relative unknowns, but who could ignore the grandeur of their proposed creation? The judges did not, and we are more than happy with the selection that gave us one of the most striking and imposing buildings any city could have. Not surprisingly, it has been granted Grade I listed status.

Below: It was at the start of the 1930s when this fleet of Midland buses, lined up opposite The Barrel Inn, left the Settlement on Summer Lane for a special outing organised by the Mothers' Union. History does not record their destination, but for many on board that would have been a matter of little importance. A day trip back then was the equivalent of a foreign holiday today for those women who found it hard to find one halfpenny to rub, never mind two. Established in 1899, the Birmingham Settlement was run by women for the benefit of mothers and children from impoverished backgrounds. At the beginning of the last century, working conditions in the mines, factories and industrial plants were still poor, despite the best efforts of many Victorian reformers. Sanitation in most working class homes left much to be desired and this combination of factors took its toll. Widows' weeds were all too frequent a sight and, in the days before the welfare state took charge, charitable support was the alternative to the workhouse. When so many husbands failed to return from the first world war their wives often found themselves in straitened circumstances without the breadwinners. With this sort of background compounded by the economic slump in the late 1920s, it is little wonder that those at the Settlement were overjoyed with something now so mundane as a day in the country or at the seaside.

Right: Brittain's Smokers' Market was a wholesale tobacco warehouse in Deritend, situated alongside a bridge over the River Rea. On 29 April 1935 lighting up a cigarette was a normal, everyday part of life. For a smart woman, a long cigarette holder clasped limply in the fingers was a sign of sophistication. The well to do males passed round the cigars with the after dinner port as the ladies left the table and others pulled happily on their briars, belching clouds of smoke from vessels packed with Gold Block. Out on the street, the lower classes puffed happily on Woodbines that they nicknamed 'coffin nails', but took little note of the significance of the soubriquet. Old men and some women favoured clay pipes and the most inveterate of smokers cut a shank of thick twist and pushed it into the bowl with a gnarled and blackened thumb. On this day, the little delivery van might have come across an invention so simple, but so effective, that was used on the roads for the first time. Percy Shaw's brainwave of cats' eyes, the manufacture of which was to make him a fortune, made their bow. His idea is one of many road safety measures introduced in the 1930s that have stood the test of time. One that was short lived saw police cars attempting to stop speeding motorists by chasing after them and banging gongs to attract attention.

Below: In the first half of the 20th century, Mitchell and Butlers rivalled Ansell's as the top midlands' brewery. The company was so well known that it was simply referred to by everyone as M & B. In truth, it was not based in Birmingham, but at Cape Hill, Smethwick, yet its Dear's Leap logo was a common enough sign on Birmingham pubs for us to regard it as our own. This promotional dray stood opposite the Union Castle Line's passenger agency on Paradise Street on 11 July 1938, offering steamship passages to such exotic destinations as East and South Africa. Henry Mitchell and William Butler,

two formerly independent brewers, founded M & B in 1875. Butler was a former hairdresser who turned to brewing when he took over the London Works Tavern, Smethwick. He had formed a friendship with Mitchell, the owner of the Old Crown Inn, when he worked there as a barman before branching out on his own. Henry Mitchell was the son of the first Henry who moved from Bromyard in the 1920s and, in 1851, took over the running of the Oddfellows Arms, West Bromwich. However, it was his son who expanded the business and was the driving force behind the company that opened the large 14 acre site at

Cape Hill in 1879. It was built on land where once deer roamed wild through a forest, hence the choice of trademark. M & B was taken over by Bass in the 1960s, but the brewery and many public houses still use the old name. Henry Mitchell was so popular in Smethwick that a park and a leisure centre both bear his name. Other Mitchells went on to achieve fame in different fields and include Sir John Mitchell, a former Recorder in Smethwick and Rye, Cedric Mitchell, a noted Pembroke architect and Andrew Mitchell, a distinguished northwest headmaster.

Above: Bank managers used to look and act like Captain Mainwaring from 'Dad's Army', with their business suits and fussy, no nonsense manner. Now, you never see them. Perhaps they no longer exist because it is impossible to speak to one. Anyone telephoning a bank in order to speak to someone in authority is in for a great disappointment as there is not a snowball's chance in the fiery furnace of being connected with the local branch. Press one for silly music, two to be told that your call is valued, three to be put in a queue, four for Dubai or Delhi and five to be cut off. In the meantime your bank has reopened as the Rat and Ferret theme bar and your funds have been laundered through someone else's slush fund. Hey-ho! It was rather different on 7 June 1939 when the manager and counter staff knew their customers personally and they could be confident that advice was soundly given and appropriate to their individual circumstances. The Old Bank, founded in 1765, was Lloyd's first in Birmingham. Here it is seen on High street, near Dale End, and viewed from the end of Carrs Lane. Not only has this bank now disappeared, so has that style of financial dealing.

Above: There was a time when teenagers actually went out for some refreshment that did not involve gallons of lager or bottles of brightly coloured and overpriced alcopops with a brawl for afters. They popped into the Milk Bar, like the one on Smallbrook Street, for a fizzy drink or cup of tea before heading off across the road and in between the A50 and A30 cars for a Friday night in the Scala. In 1956 they would have enjoyed one of the best movies ever made. Of course it never won an Oscar, nor were any of those involved even considered for an Academy Award that year. 'The Searchers', easily director John Ford's most influential film, gave cinema audiences a Western that had more about it than baddies in black hats and six shooters. The story line of a man looking for his kidnapped niece also included the themes of racism and obsession. John Wayne brilliantly played a role that was way beyond his usual gung-ho rubbish. As they munched their Payne's Poppets on the back row the teenagers remarked on the pretty girl who played the part of the youngster in the clutch of the Red Indians and wondered if this Natalie Wood that they had never heard of would ever be seen again. The conversation was brief as the usherette shushed them, so they returned to smooching with their beaus. That got the usherette going again and she shone her torch their way. The Scala closed in 1960 and was replaced by the Odeon. George Hall is in the distance, ready for demolition.

Below: The Guinness slogan, that it 'is good for you', was used as long ago as 1951. It still pops up from time to time over half a century later. If you have a memorable catchphrase, why not milk it? In that era, going to the pictures was one of the high spots of the week's entertainment. Hardly any homes had television, so the silver screen had little in the way of competition when providing escapism for the masses. What good value for money we had as well. There were usually two films in every programme, though it must be said that the supporting feature was often quite a dire 'B' movie and probably starred Ronald Reagan. We also got a Tom and Jerry cartoon, some sort of quasi educational item about travel or light engineering that saw a mass exodus to the toilet and Pathé News. That last screening was very popular. Everyone sat up to take notice as the cockerel crowed its overture to the only moving picture information to which we had access. West End Cinema, on Suffolk Street, had previously been the Curzon Hall when it opened on 9 March 1925. Designed by Frederick Pepper, the proscenium arch was surrounded by delightful stained glass panels that had been created by the Bromsgrove Guild. Cinemas built in the first third of the last century were works of art as well as places of entertainment. The West End closed in March 1967 and was demolished as the road was widened.

Once upon a time, Queen Victoria had the company of her beloved consort, Prince Albert in the middle of the square named for her. Today, she has to stand alone. This part of the city has been out of bounds to traffic for some time, but in the earlier years of the last century cars could come and go as they pleased. The word 'pedestrianised' had not even been coined and 'traffic calming measures' would have brought a puzzled frown to the brow. That latter phrase draws a similar response from modern motorists who find it difficult to understand how a nice wide road can be improved by narrowing it with a mixture of white paint and concrete bollards. Calming is not the word used to describe the effect upon drivers who have just had their suspension ruptured by humps placed in the middle of the carriageway by someone probably sponsored by a repair centre. The scene beyond the Town Hall, on the left, has changed radically as the buildings on Edmund Street were gutted and, eventually, the Adrian Boult Centre and new Central Library appeared. The 1885 museum and art gallery clock tower, though, still peeks over the Council House, once Birmingham's largest building. Yeoville Thomason designed both buildings, with the latter opening in 1878.

Left: A cold, late autumnal day greeted the students of King Edward's School on New Street on 27 November 1935. They were probably too young to have noticed what one or two of their masters who supported the sport of kings had realised, that today was Steve Donoghue's last race. The man who had been champion jockey many times over and who rode a hat trick of Derby winners in the early 1920s, finally called it a day. The school itself would not long survive the famous little man, not on New Street, that is. It was demolished the following year and the staff and pupils moved to new premises on the Bristol Road, Edgbaston. The old school was designed by Sir Charles Barry (1795-1860), a major influence in the Gothic revival school of architecture that saw him lead the building of the Houses of Parliament (1840-60). The Church of Saint Peter at Brighton (1826) and the Travellers' Club in Pall Mall (1831) were features of his earlier work. In 1833, King Edward's Grammar School was completed on the east side of New Street. It continued the educational tradition established on 2 January 1552 when the school was established in the former guild building. By the late 17th century, 200 boys were passing through the doors, in addition to those in the 'petty' school, a form of preparatory. One headmaster of the early 19th century revelled in the name of 'Butcher' Cooke. More recent old boys include Enoch Powell, Ken Tynan and cricketers Ossie Wheatley, Alan Smith and Mark Wagh.

Above: Work on Victoria Square's Town Hall began in 1832, five years before the great lady ascended to the throne and long in advance of the more modern naming of this spot. Designed by Joseph Aloysius Hansom and Edward Welch, it is probably Britain's finest example of a recreation of a Roman temple. In this instance, it was modelled on the one of Castor and Pollux, the mythological Gemini twins, in the Roman Forum. Certainly, the delightfully moulded Corinthian porticos and the colonnades create an almost authentic effect of classical work. Quite why anyone should wish to mount a television screen on the side that faces into Chamberlain Square, so that sandwich eaters sitting on the steps outside the library can gawp at the lunchtime news, remains an aesthetic mystery. The only wonder is that it has not looked for sponsorship and been renamed the Pizza Hut Town Hall or Reebok House. It looked beautiful as it was, so why not leave well alone? The single flag flying above the roof in this c1957 photograph was a sufficient addition. To the left, we can just see the Chamberlain Memorial fountain, erected in memory of the former Birmingham mayor and MP. The unrelated JH Chamberlain designed it, with additional sculpture work by Thomas Woolner.

With words such as 'It will all be over by Christmas', young mums with their new born babies left their homes in early September on their way to billets in homes far away from the threat of the onslaught from the skies that they feared would come. They were loath to leave their husbands and familiar surroundings, but the maternal instinct was stronger than any marriage vow. Tears were shed, but it was a case of better safe than sorry. The official with the clipboard had little time to spare on sentimentality. His job was to tick them off his list, get them on board and have them whisked away to safety in the countryside or to some small town that did not have the sort of heavy industry or military importance that would attract the attention of the enemy. The police were hard pressed in keeping the long lines moving, but they did so with a mixture of efficiency and concern. Elsewhere, pregnant women and the very aged and infirm were also evacuated and not just for their safety. Should the bombs come raining down, then their lack of mobility would become a liability in an emergency. Some teachers took advantage of the evacuation qualification rules as they would be wanted in schools where increased pupil numbers created a need. However, many refused the opportunity, preferring to stay at home with their own loved ones or to offer their services to king and country.

Above: This c1960 view of the clock tower on the Museum and Art Gallery could not be witnessed today. The block of buildings dominating Edmund Street have been swept away as the area was redeveloped into Chamberlain Square and the Adrian Boult Hall was built. Edmund Street is now restricted to the part that runs from the archway next to the tower and along to Snow Hill Station. The street was renamed in 1778 from Harlow Street in honour of Edmund Colmore, a member of the once influential family of mercers. Edmund Street was once an important terminus for buses to Smethwick and Dudley, but was one of the victims when Paradise Circus was built. The Hope and Anchor pub was a popular watering hole, well frequented by Council House staff as well as shoppers in the city centre. It was part of the Ansell chain, one of the two most influential local brewers of the early 20th century. Joseph Ansell founded the company in 1857. Ansell and Son were originally maltsters and hop merchants, but moved into brewing in 1881, registering as a limited company eight years later. The acquisition of Holt's in 1934 made it one of the largest regional breweries in Britain. The merger with Ind Coope and Tetley Walker to form Allied Breweries in 1961 marked the beginning of the end for its independent soul. The brewery at Aston Cross closed 20 years later and brewing moved to Burton on Trent, though the trade name has been retained under the Carlsberg Tetley banner.

Like some scene from 'The Godfather', a horse's head can be seen at the bottom right of the picture. Fortunately, we can rest assured that the remainder of it was still attached as it pulled a cart along Broad Street in the direction of the city centre in 1934. The young girls on the left may well be great grandmothers by now and, if still in Birmingham, will have witnessed many changes to the style of buildings along here. Later ones came as a result of city architects and planners meeting the needs of modern society, but the first catalyst was as a result of Hermann Goering's Luftwaffe. During World War II, the many air raids on our city left Broad Street looking rather woebegone in the aftermath of the rain of death that came down from the skies as Junkers and Dorniers unleashed their loads of high explosive. Most of the properties along here were affected and many, including the Prince of Wales theatre and Bingley Hall, were devastated. Even now, over 60 years on, our little girls will have vivid recollections of those scenes. Broad Street was still regarded, at the time of this photograph, as being somewhat superior, linking the city, as it did, with a somewhat posher Edgbaston. However, those looking behind the shops would discover some rather squalid hovels masquerading as homes. Major redevelopment began in the mid 1980s, bringing hotels, the International Convention Centre, Symphony Hall and Centenary Square to life as Broad Street's persona changed completely.

There were times when it appeared that Broad Street was just as busy with traffic as it is today. In 1936, the volume of cars and buses must have made the workman's position on the ladder a rather precarious one as he attended to the ornate streetlight. The bus heading his way was a Daimler COG5 on the route to Acocks Green, to the southeast of the city. The cars seem to be complying with the Henry Ford mantra of 'any colour you like, as long as it is black'. The new showroom at the bottom right corner with Berkley Street would open as Osler's, the electric light manufacturer. Today it is home to a large hotel, part of the chain of Jury's Inns. The Grosvenor Workman shop on the opposite side of Berkley Street sold garden ornaments, fencing, wheelbarrows and similar equipment. In later years

it was taken over by Philip Fyne's car dealership, rivalling the trade carried out from Reeves and Stedeford's Sunbeam and Singer agency across Broad Street, on the corner of Oozells Street. After the Berkley Street corner was redeveloped, Allied Carpets and Ronnie Scott's Jazz Club were to be found here. However, the Rocket Club now occupies the Grosvenor Workman site, while R & S is home to Vodafone. The shadow cast at the entrance to Oozells Street was made by the Second Church of Christ Scientist and the building is still intact, though no longer a religious establishment, and is now used as Flares' club. Looking northeast down Broad Street, the keen eyed might be able to make out the Crown, the Prince of Wales theatre, Bingley Hall and the Brasshouse, as well as the more obvious Church of the Messiah.

Above: The old Central Library was a grand imposing building, with its ornate architecture that included carved colonnades, fine buttresses and a handsome portico. Designed by EM Barry, it adjoined the Midland Institute and extended from Edmund Street to Paradise Street and became the largest lending library in the country. Birmingham's fathers took an interest in library provision following the 1850 Act of Parliament that granted local authorities the right to establish public libraries. Some of the more reactionary among leading figures of the time worried that greater access to learning and information for the masses might provide a basis for even greater insurrection than had been seen during the Chartist riots and the burgeoning trade union movement that led to the experiences of the Tolpuddle martyrs. A poll of the burgesses in 1852 did not achieve the required majority, but the social reformers had their way when the plan to introduce a public lending library was adopted on 21 February 1860. It opened on Constitution Hill on 6 September 1865, with a reference section appearing on 26 October 1866. This was destroyed in a fire on 11 January 1879 and a completely new lending and reference library opened its doors on 1 June 1882. Martin and Chamberlain, who had also worked on the original building, designed the interior. The demand for books was so overwhelming that, by the turn of the century, the number on the shelves went well into six figures. The building closed in 1973 and was demolished during the regeneration phase of that era.

Right: On 27 July 1957, near Five Ways, this top end of Broad Street still had many small, specialised shops, although it also included famous high street names such as Boot's chemists. We have all become so used to shopping in supermarkets

that provide food, clothing, electrical goods, gardening and household items, newspapers, petrol et al that we have forgotten how we or our parents used to shop. Retail outlets that were ironmongers, haberdashers, milliners and tobacconists have largely disappeared. Even some of the words used to describe these shops seem archaic. Yet, they provided the sort of individual attention and advice that no spotty shelf stacker can hope to match. Nuts, bolts and screws could be weighed out by the ounce and even sold in tiny lots, rather than the prepackaged amounts, always too many for our needs, that we have to suffer now. You could get a short piece of elastic to repair a hair band without having to purchase a yard, sorry metre, of the stuff. Even to a non smoker, the delightful aroma of thick twist or Balkan Sobranie wafting through a doorway was one of the pleasures of walking along the pavement. The factory, just visible to the right, also had its own particular attraction, as this was the site where Kunzle's delicious cakes and chocolates were manufactured. Confectionery shops used to sell misshapes that were cheap, but no less mouth watering

Below: The reader would have to be approaching middle age to have even a childhood memory of Broad Street Corner as it was at Easy Row in 1962. This was just a few years before the whole site was bulldozed and cleared for redevelopment with such buildings as the ATV centre. Over 40 years ago we could even park our cars at the side of the road without causing congestion and the number of vehicles on view shows that, even as the swinging 60s were in their infancy, there was still space round the prettily laid out roundabout and time for pedestrians to stroll over the zebra crossings. At this time, Bernard Cribbins had a top ten hit with 'Hole in the ground', a ditty about a man digging for no real purpose. Before long, teams of workmen would move in with a true aim of altering the face of the city here and elsewhere. A modern look was needed, but we lost much of the character of such spots as this in the name of progress. The change in outlook, both physical and mental, is quite dramatic as we compare this with the hurly burly of underground walkways and highway interchanges that are in and around this spot today. The photograph was taken looking towards Suffolk Street, with Congreve Street and Paradise Street on the left. The mighty structure dominating the centre of the scene belonged to the Britannic Assurance Company that later moved its premises to Moseley.

In the late evening Broad Street is a lively bustle with people patronising restaurants, bars, clubs and hotels in addition to those attending the International Convention Centre. These activities epitomise the aspect of Birmingham's recent regeneration that has seen the shift towards service industries in more recent years. However, in the early part of the last century it was a lot different, as we can see from the individual shops on the street as boneshakers of cars rattle by, weaving past the standard perilously placed in the centre of the carriageway. Delightfully-wrought lamp standards dotted the pavements and life was conducted underneath them at a pace that would be far too sedate for modern society as it rushes pell-mell on its pursuit of pleasure and monetarism. The road developed from what was a mere narrow track that ran along a ridge, passing through the Islington estate from Bewdley Street, later to be reconstructed as Victoria Square, and on down to Five Ways. The Birmingham end of the track was widened in the late 18th century, hence its name, to become an important highway lined by elegant houses. Tollgates were erected separating the town from Edgbaston until the early Victorian era. By the middle of the 19th century, housing on the south side of Broad Street appeared as the town grew in size when the influence of the industrial revolution encouraged people living in rural communities to seek work in large conurbations. The houses, though, were cramped, insanitary affairs and these back to back terraces were a breeding ground for disease. Despite this, some were still inhabited as late as the early 1960s.

Events & occasions

Here in New Street the shops have their striped awnings out providing shade from the bright spring sunshine. It's May in 1937. It is not however an average May: as can be seen from this view taken from Marshal and Snelgrove looking towards the High Street the flags are out for a special occasion. The event was the unexpected coronation of George VI. Some £15,000 was allocated by the council to mark the occasion. Half a crown (12 1/2p) was given to everyone over the age of 65 not receiving a pension, whilst every child born on Coronation Day itself, 12th May, would receive a whole pound. Every secondary school child was allocated just over one shilling (5p) and there were souvenir mugs and tins of chocolate for younger school children. Those who didn't benefit from personal gifts could share in the collective celebrations. The council provided funds for decorations, fireworks, concerts and even an illuminated tramcar. The 1937 coronation would be the last great public celebration before the outbreak of the second world war. For many however it was an event tinged with puzzlement. Why was King George the king at all? Why had his elder brother felt it necessary to abdicate from the throne in 1936 to be with the woman he loved - simply because she had been divorced? Self imposed censorship by the media had ensured that the British public were the last in the world to know about Edward's relationship with Mrs Simson.

Above: A traffic policeman wearing a white helmet and coat tells us that something unusual is in the offing. That something was Birmingham's coronation parade on 12th May 1937. The parade included representatives from the Royal Navy, the Seaforth Highlanders, the Territorial Army, the Auxiliary Air Force as well as firemen and nurses, the St John's Ambulance Brigade in addition to the officer training corps from Birmingham University. Some 150 veterans of the Boer war also marched past, as did more than 300 Old Contemptibles from the first world war. Elsewhere in the city there were band concerts in 21 parks whilst church bells rang almost incessantly. The St John's Ambulance folk and those nurses had to get back to work pretty soon: one of the unexpected consequences of the coronation was the large number of elderly people taken to hospital after they had broken their legs taking part in street races after 'celebrating' too enthusiastically. Thousands of folk now getting well on in years will recall attending the big parade: rather more of course remember the street parties afterwards where they toasted the health of the King and Queen in lemonade. One aspect about the whole proceedings however that seems very odd to us today is not seeing the actual event. Sixteen years later many folk would see Queen Elizabeth II's coronation live on television: in 1937 those who wanted to see what happened in London either had to be there or wait for the Pathé News at the cinema.

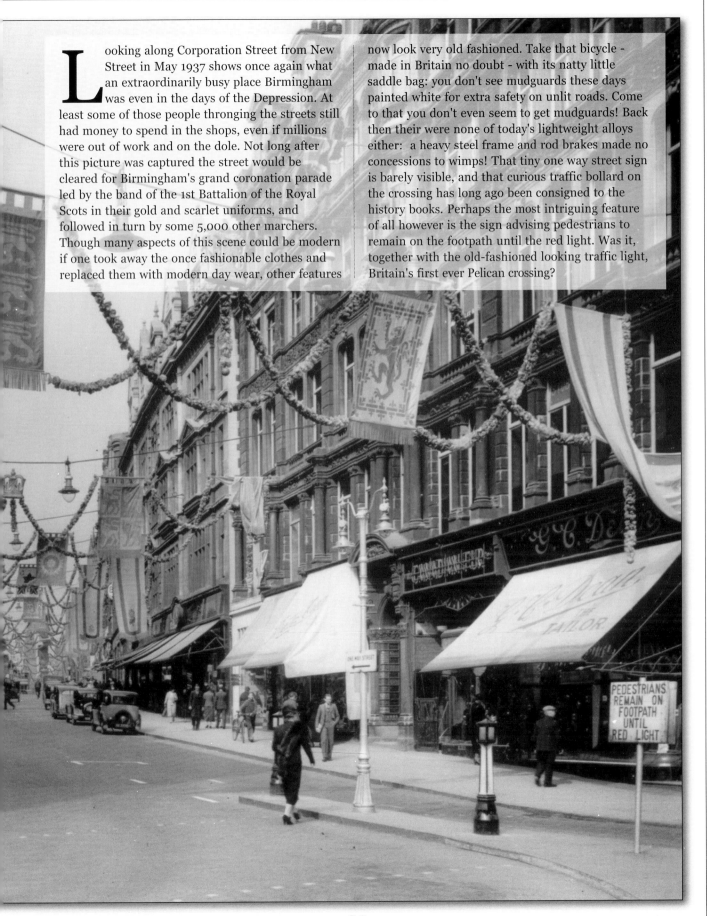

ooking along Corporation Street from New Street in May 1937 shows once again what an extraordinarily busy place Birmingham was even in the days of the Depression. At least some of those people thronging the streets still had money to spend in the shops, even if millions were out of work and on the dole. Not long after this picture was captured the street would be cleared for Birmingham's grand coronation parade led by the band of the 1st Battalion of the Royal Scots in their gold and scarlet uniforms, and followed in turn by some 5,000 other marchers. Though many aspects of this scene could be modern if one took away the once fashionable clothes and replaced them with modern day wear, other features now look very old fashioned. Take that bicycle - made in Britain no doubt - with its natty little saddle bag: you don't see mudguards these days painted white for extra safety on unlit roads. Come to that you don't even seem to get mudguards! Back then their were none of today's lightweight alloys either: a heavy steel frame and rod brakes made no concessions to wimps! That tiny one way street sign is barely visible, and that curious traffic bollard on the crossing has long ago been consigned to the history books. Perhaps the most intriguing feature of all however is the sign advising pedestrians to remain on the footpath until the red light. Was it, together with the old-fashioned looking traffic light, Britain's first ever Pelican crossing?

Shopping arcades were an early feature of Birmingham life - so much so that the 'Mail' described it as an 'Arcadian town' as far back as 1882. People are invited to 'Wander Round the Arcade' at Allans. In the distance the Beehive proudly advertises its Preedy's Curly Cut tobacco alongside Preedy's QED. Fifty years later the view would show Dorothy Perkins instead of Allans and the Gas Showrooms further down the street. The High Street is pictured here in 1946. The uniforms seen along the pavement to the left, along with the sign for the Air Raid Precaution shelter, remind us that the war had not long been concluded, though the most prominent figure in uniform, with double-breasted brass buttons, looks to be a fireman rather than a member of the armed forces. And what about that No Entry sign on the left? Drivers today travel so quickly they would barely have the chance to spot this all but invisible bit of 'road furniture'. But these were the days when it was still possible to drive through Birmingham at a leisurely pace and, with no double yellow lines, park your car right outside the shop of your choice. Or at least that was so for the lucky few who actually owned a car. For most folk it was a case of getting the bus then walking. Perhaps the most remarkable thing about this scene is the number of people strolling in road - these days if you survived the danger you'd get arrested for jaywalking.

Above: Victoria Square looked very pretty on 1 June 1953, the eve of the coronation of Queen Elizabeth II. Floral arrangements were in place, bunting, streamers and the royal coat of arms hung from the Town Hall and other municipal buildings as the nation prepared for the great day. It was to be the first major national celebration since VJ Day in August 1945 and everyone was ready to have a ball. The sun shone brightly as little knots of people discussed how they were going to celebrate the special day. The city centre would see processions and fine speeches, but pride of place eventually was awarded to the humble back streets where wonderful street parties were held. Unfortunately, the previous day's sun stubbornly refused to shine and stayed behind leaden skies for most of the day. It even dared to pour with rain in the capital city, but no one's spirits were dampened. The gaiety of the occasion outdid the worst of the weather and, for those lucky enough to see a little flickering black and white television picture enhanced by a Richard Dimbleby commentary, who can forget Queen Salote? The sight of this large, beaming figure from Tonga, waving frenetically to the crowds as her carriage filled with rainwater, was one of the defining memories of the day.

Above: Elizabeth Cadbury (1858-1951) married George, one of the founders of the Cadbury Brothers empire, in 1888. She was particularly interested in the welfare of young people and dedicated much of her life to the YWCA, Girl Guides and the Union of Girls' Clubs. She was also heavily involved in local hospitals and medical services and somehow found time to support the Liberal party, the work of the League of Nations, serve as a city councillor and perform the duties as a magistrate. Despite all the various strings to her considerable bow, her enduring commitment was to youngsters. As chairman of the Bournville Village Trust, she was still involved with this VJ Day party held on 15 August 1945, despite being in her late 80s. Over 100 little ones, seated at trestle tables adorned with Union flags, had been well scrubbed up to enjoy the grub that the mums and trustees had provided to celebrate the end of the war with Japan. A similar scene took place three months earlier when hostilities in Europe came to an end, but it took the bombing of Nagasaki and Hiroshima to encourage Emperor Hirohito's surrender. The festivities were tinged with sadness because some of the children knew that daddy would never be coming home.

Above: Among the men, it is simple to pick out the bosses from the workers. A glance at their headwear is all that is required. Flat caps versus bowlers make it a doddle to decide which ones held the reins of power. Oddly, though, the rest of the apparel was quite similar. When not in their work clothes, the lower classes favoured jackets and trousers, just like their better heeled managers and employers, even if the cut of their jib was decidedly less expensive. Quite a few also sported ties, though those who opted for mufflers rather gave the social strata game away. The fleet of wagons on view in this c1930 scene belonged to the Delta Metals Company and were filled with youngsters about to enjoy their day out. The Ashtead's children's outing was partly organised by the vicar of the Church of St Laurence, seen with his coat over his arm. The transport may not have been comfortable and modern liberals might comment on the cattle truck analogy but, to poor kids during the depression years, this was the equivalent of a fortnight in Benidorm. Fathers were out of work and bread and dripping was a feast, so a few aches and pains from a bumpy ride was the least of their worries. During this era, parents were only too glad to take advantage of anything from donations of children's clothing to free tea parties at the local church hall.

Looking across Victoria Square towards the central building of J Lyons and Company, the clock reached 12.30 pm as the Lords Mayor read the proclamation of Queen Elizabeth's accession to the throne on 8 February 1952, just 48 hours after her father's death. When his funeral took place just seven days after this scene was enacted, three British queens were in attendance. George's wife, Elizabeth, who was to survive as the 'Queen Mum' for another 50 years, the new monarch and his mother, Mary, widow of George V, formed an unhappy trio in the cortege that paid its last respects. Queen Mary's heart must have been broken as this was the third of her sons that she had buried. The sickly John died as a teenager in 1919 and George, Duke of Kent perished in a plane crash in 1942. Mary passed away the following year, still grieving. The crowds in Victoria Square to listen to the proclamation overflowed down Colmore Row, Waterloo Street and New Street, as far as the eye could see. The central figure of Victoria was made from a bronze cast of the original marble statue that was erected on 10 January 1901, just before the old lady passed away. Princess Elizabeth unveiled the replacement in 1951. The modern Victoria Square was opened by Diana, Princess of Wales on 6 May 1993 and now forms part of the continuous paved walkway that takes you from the International Convention Centre to New Street.

Below: The Lord Mayor led the service at this gathering of the armed forces held in Victoria Square in the early 1940s. His rallying cry to the troops from the temporary stage echoed around the square via the tannoys relaying his message that was a mixture of exhortation to action and painful memory of those who had already made the ultimate sacrifice. It was important for the general public to see their boys at close quarters so that they could give them thanks at first hand for all they were doing in defence of the realm. It also acted as a wake up call to those yet to volunteer and as a warning to those who were careless in the way they lived their lives. A banner on the Post Office read 'Kill the Squanderbug', reminding everyone to conserve valuable and scarce materials that could be used in the war effort. It was not just the boys in service that the public observed in this rally. There were girls in uniform, too. Army women were part of the Auxiliary Territorial Service and, by July 1942, their ranks numbered 217,000. Those with a love of aeroplanes were assigned to the Women's Auxiliary Air Force and, although forbidden to fly warplanes, were invaluable as radar operatives. Budding mariners joined the Women's Royal Naval Service. The so-called weaker sex also donned uniforms at home by joining any of a host of civil defence organisations.

Above: New Street Station has seen many important visitors walk along its platforms, but there are few as prestigious as those who belong to the royal family. Love them or hate them, they are news. When George VI was our monarch, the feelings were much warmer then than they are in the 21st century, although it must be said that most of the negative comments are reserved for the present Queen's relatives rather than directly for her. There was little in the way of anti monarchist feeling to be found when this royal train arrived. Some station staff climbed up on top of counters, or any other vantage point, to get a glimpse of the couple whose popularity was never in question. King George (1895-1952) had been thrust into the limelight in late 1936 when his brother, Edward VIII, abdicated. Britons warmed to a man who was shy and retiring, unlike his brasher, socialite predecessor. They also approved of his wife, the former Elizabeth Bowes Lyon (1900-2002), as she was British, unlike the succession of foreign consorts previous kings and queens had foisted upon them. Cynics remarked that anything was better than the twice divorced American we might have had, but George and Elizabeth really made their mark during the war. They stayed when many might have run to the safety of Canada or some other haven. The British never forgot that and, as a result, loved them all the more.

Below: Cadbury is a famous midlands name and there is not a soul in the land who has not enjoyed the confectionery that has tickled our palates for over a century. Cadbury's made its first chocolate bar in 1897, using fresh milk to give it a lighter, creamier look than other chocolates. Dairy Milk soon became a best seller. When Queen Elizabeth II and the Duke of Edinburgh received a rapturous welcome from the workers at Bournville in 1955, following the royal couple's brief stop at the Concert Hall, they soon discovered that the Cadbury history went back much further than its renowned chocolate bar. John Cadbury was a coffee and tea merchant in the early 19th century and passed on his firm to his sons, George and Richard, in 1861. By 1866, Cadbury Brothers, as the company became known, became the first to sell cocoa in powder form that could be made into a nourishing drink. As business expanded, the company moved out of Birmingham to larger and healthier premises at Bournville, named after the small stream that ran through the site. George Cadbury (1839-1922), though the younger brother, was the driving force. His was a Quaker family, coincidentally as were Fry and Rowntree, and he had a firm belief in looking after the welfare of others. He also was cute enough to know that happy employees made good ones and built houses for his workers, grouping them together to create a community feel.

Transport

Below: When it was reconstructed between 1906 and 1912 its booking hall was one of the distinguishing features which gave Snow Hill railway station a reputation as one of the finest on the Great Western network. Snow Hill opened in 1852; the Great Western Hotel being added to it in 1863. In 1967 however the station lost its main line status when, following electrification, services were concentrated at New Street. Snow Hill's great days were over, though local services to Wolverhampton continued from there until 1972 when the station was finally closed to passenger traffic. Today, in a world dominated by cars and where travel by air is something most people have experienced it's hard to explain the importance the railways once had. Travelling by rail was by far the quickest way to travel when cars rarely exceeded 40 miles per hour. And, except in the engine of an ocean going liner, where could one see such raw power? A steam locomotive was huge, man-made dragon, a living breathing beast that hissed and smoked and spat sparks into the night, tamed only by might and skill. No wonder every boy had the ambition to be an engine driver. Here we can see Platform 7. Destination boards atop the carriages and the sight of porters ready to help passengers with their luggage is a sure indicator that this scene was captured for posterity before Dr Beeching's penny pinching axe bit deep into Britain's rail network in the early 1960s.

Above: Those of us with thickening waistlines and greying locks think that we remember hordes of conductresses on Midland Red buses. Nostalgia is not necessarily an accurate guide to fact. 'Clippies', as they were fondly called, were relatively rare as few females were employed in public transport in 1953. Dot Anderson was one of a small band, but somehow we have come to associate her role as being synonymous of the era. Despite that correction, everything else in this photograph is a true reflection of a scene from just over 50 years ago. Dot's hand cranked ticket machine is a lovely period piece, along with the punch used to clip the tickets, hence her job's nickname. Smokers congregated on the top deck and Dot could safely walk the aisles with her moneybag carelessly draped across her shoulder. She was never in fear of hooligans mugging her or being the subject of abuse. The worst she had to deal with was when some wag asked her, 'How far can I go for fourpence?' She just grinned and took it in her stride. Even her Christian name is a perfect period piece. There were countless Dorothys, Doreens, Sheilas and Mavises in the 1950s. They usually married an Eric, Ernest, Geoffrey or Trevor.

Below: The mid 1960s was a time of notoriety on the railways for one particular man. Dr Richard Beeching was appointed as the senior advise to the government on reshaping British Rail by improving its efficiency. The former chairman of ICI published 'The Reshaping of the Railways', a polite title for the recommendation to close and scrap many services. His 1963 report recommended shutting down 2,128 stations, cutting the rail network by 25 per cent, taking 8,000 carriages out of service and axing 67,700 jobs. Beeching even proposed closing Ballater, a station on the Balmoral line often used by the royal family. Cries of 'off with his head' echoed around humble homes as well as castles and palaces as a furore broke out. Despite the objections, Alec Douglas Home's government accepted the report and its proposals in March 1964. By the end of the year, Harold Wilson was in 10 Downing Street and Dr Beeching was shown the door. Despite his exit, the Beeching formula was introduced during 1965. Snow Hill Station, photographed on 28 May 1965 at the Colmore Row entrance, was in decline at this time. By 1967, its days as a mainline link with the Paddington Station, London over the former Great Western Railway route were virtually over as through traffic ceased to use its facilities.

Above: We can be absolutely positive that the chap on the second cart, bearing the number 31, was not speaking on a mobile phone! This was 1936, after all, and the hand up towards his mouth was probably holding a cigarette. Nowadays, of course, he would be whizzing down Broad Street in a BMW and gabbling away while attempting to steer and shift gear with one hand, oblivious to the law on such things. The horses and drivers, possibly part of a parade, were passing close to Sherborne Wharf on the Worcester and Birmingham Canal. The building on the left is the Brasshouse, now a pub and restaurant. Its original use is obvious from the name and dates from 1781 when 200 merchants, tired of the inflationary prices charged for brass, decided to contribute the not inconsiderable sum of £100 each to manufacture their own supplies. The favourable location by the canal was helpful in gaining easy access to markets beyond the town boundaries. The Brasshouse continued in business until the middle of the 19th century when it was sold to the Waterworks Company. It was later to be used by the Weights and Measures Department and has also seen service as a base for the Samaritans and as an adult education centre. The Unitarian Church in the photograph was erected in 1862, though we would hope that baptisms were carried out using font water rather than that gathered from the canal over which it was built! Joseph Chamberlain (1836-1914), whose pioneer efforts in educational reform, slum clearance, improved housing and municipalisation of public utilities endeared him to the Birmingham masses, was a regular worshipper here.

Below: Looking very modern, the two young women on the right were quite daring in their fashion selection. Their hair was cut short and they favoured trousers rather than dresses or blouses and skirts. The older generation, represented by the woman behind them, did not approve of such casual attire, especially when out and about in the city. Those ladies of certain years knew that a hat was essential, gloves a must, stockinged legs de rigueur and the ubiquitous handbag a permanent accessory. What was the world coming to when young women looked like the men they were supposed to be trying to attract? Heaven forbid, but some of them might even not want to become housewives! Whatever next? The youth of today! It is amusing how often that phrase has been repeated down the

years and, dare we suggest, by this same pair as they reached middle age. On Monday, 30 May 1955 they were not concerned with matters of decorum as they read the special notices board at Snow Hill Station. A national railway strike had been called and only a skeleton service was being run. This industrial action was partly in support of fellow trades unionists and was during a period of crisis for the government. Anthony Eden had only just replaced Winston Churchill as prime minister and was immediately faced with a month long strike of newspaper workers, followed by a rail strike earlier than the one that affected Snow Hill in this photograph. Dockworkers withdrew their labour for six weeks and the Home Secretary, Major Lloyd George, declared a state of emergency.

Above: Birmingham was granted its first market charter in 1166. Exactly 800 years later the ancient site of that market underwent a radical change. Work on the new Bull Ring which began in 1961 would destroy almost every vestige of this part of the city's past even more effectively than had the Luftwaffe. The completion of the ring road, constructed between 1967 and 1971, with its concrete bridges, walkways and underpasses would additionally remove all traces of the Market Hall, the large building in the centre of this scene, which had been built in 1835. What had once been Birmingham's village green, where farmers from the surrounding countryside sold their produce and offered their flocks of sheep and herds of cattle for sale, was, alas, now far from being green. Change to the urban landscape was of course nothing new. The FW Woolworth store on the left had appeared only in the first half 20th century; the American company had opened its first British store in Liverpool in 1909. Within two decades no British town or city was compete without its branch of 'Woolies'. Though the old Market Hall may have passed into history its successors survived in the shape of the Bull Ring Centre whose indoor market has no fewer than 90 stalls, whilst St Martin's in the centre of the Bull Ring provided 400 pitches for jewellery, crafts, household goods and clothes in an atmosphere which would not have seemed alien to those original shoppers back in the 12th century.

A century of car manufacturing at Longbridge

2005 marked the centenary of car manufacturing at Longbridge, in South Birmingham. Over the last 100 years, Longbridge was at the centre of the evolution in the motor industry, but back in 1905 a pioneer of the motoring age simply had one desire.

'Most everything worthwhile is born of some dreamers dream' were the words held dear to Herbert Austin, whose dream was to make motorcars. That foresighted belief continues today, with the Longbridge site operating in independent ownership as MG Rover Group. However back in a time before 1894, the original Longbridge site was purely agricultural with only one house, called 'The Wonders', situated in the area of today's Car Assembly Building (CAB) 1.

Top: Herbert Austin, founder of the Austin Motor Company.
Below: The first Austin car in 1906 with Herbert Austin driving. Right: The 15 HP Norfolk Single Laudaulet of 1909.

On March 19, 1894, building began of a factory for a Birmingham printing company, White and Pike Ltd. The factory was for a new venture - making and printing tin boxes. By around 1901, however, the business was abandoned.

Herbert Austin and all three of the staff of the Austin Motor Company explored the area around Birmingham on November 4, 1905 in his Wolseley 7.5hp. With a picnic basket strapped to

200,000 sold. In 1926, extensions to the factory brought the plant size up to 62 acres. By this time, Longbridge had become a self contained manufacturing plant, with its own foundry, forge, press shops, power station and paint plants, in addition to engine, bodyshell and final assembly facilities. But even at this time, internal works transport at Longbridge still used a number of wagons drawn by shire horses, accommodated in the factory stables!

the car, they discovered the disused but well located and modern White and Pike Printing Works. Declaring to himself that it would be the perfect location for a vehicle factory, his staff moved in later that week and Austin formerly became its owner on January 22, 1906.

By February 1906, the first chassis was road tested, going on to become the first complete car, an Austin Endcliffe 25/30 hp Phaeton estate with four speed gearbox and chain drive rear axle. In its first year, Longbridge had produced 23 cars, quite an achievement given the challenges and the novelty of the motorcar.

Four 100hp cars were developed for the 1908 French Grand Prix. Two of these became the only British cars to finish the race in 15th and 16th positions and one of them survived to become a star exhibit at the Heritage Motor Centre, at Gaydon.

But in 1914 when the Great War broke out, Longbridge converted its production to war armaments. Eight million shells, 650 guns, nearly 500 armoured cars, ambulances and pumping equipment were produced. By 1917, the Longbridge site had trebled in size. A new munitions plant and an aircraft flying ground were added. During this busy time, a civilian aircraft with folding wings, the Austin Whippet, was produced, with a choice of three or five cylinder Anzani radial engines. In the same year, Herbert Austin was knighted in recognition of Longbridge's contribution to the war effort.

The Seven Horse, introduced in 1922 was launched as Austin's 'Motor for the Millions' and was very popular, with over

Top: Austin 18-24 Tourer 1912 pictured outside the Longbridge Sales Office in 1930. **Right:** Sir Herbert Austin in his robe as Lord Austin Baron of Longbridge.

Prior to the massive expansion of the factory in the late 1930s, part of the spare land at Longbridge was utilised as a farm. Longbridge built tractors were demonstrated to potential customers alongside the Austin cars. These were also built under licence in France by Societe Anonyne Austin in Lioncourt.

By 1930, weekly production at Longbridge reached a record 1,000 units. Four years later, there were 44 separate models of Austin vehicles available, based on nine types of chassis. When combined with colour and option choices, this gave a total of 333 distinct permutations.

In 1936 Sir Herbert Austin became Lord Austin Baron of Longbridge in recognition of his support for the Cavendish Laboratory, Cambridge, where his friend, Lord Rutherford,

succeeded in splitting the atom. During this year, Lord Austin became Chairman of the Government shadow factory scheme to build aircraft and aero engines. Barely had the new Austin 12hp been launched when war was declared and once more Longbridge was converted to military production. Some 36,000 war-effort vehicles from

8hp utility pick-ups to four-wheel drive military trucks and ambulances were built. 100,000 suspension and drive gear units for Churchill Tanks were developed, 2.5 million ammunition boxes created, over 1.25 million piercing shells produced and around half a million steel helmets.

Building of the first shadow factory (now known as the East Works) had commenced in Longbridge in 1936. The factory began with a contract to produce 900 Fairey Battle aircraft over three years. By the end of the war, Longbridge had produced nearly 3,000 aircraft including Hurricanes, Stirling and Lancaster Bombers. Many of these were flown directly from the factory, but the Stirling and Lancaster Bombers were taken to Elmdon for final assembly.

Following a daytime raid on Longbridge, Lord Austin attended the funeral of those killed. While there, he caught double pneumonia from which he never recovered. He died on May 23, 1941.

Leonard Lord became chairman and managing director in November 1945. By 1946, the millionth Longbridge car had been produced and two years later the total export earnings at Longbridge reached over £30 million annually.

In 1952, Austin merged with the Nuffield Organisation and Longbridge became the headquarters of the new British Motor Corporation (BMC). Agreement was also reached with Donald Healey to produce the Austin Healey 100 sports car at Longbridge.

1953 marked the second millionth Longbridge car produced. Two years on, the company celebrated 50 years at Longbridge and Lord laid the foundation stone for the new sales block and exhibition hall. Lord planned the 1950s to be an exciting decade at Longbridge and indeed it was. The A series engine increased in size from 803cc to 948cc for the new A35 and Minor 1000 models.

The Mini was launched on August 26, 1959. As BMC had been formed by the merger of the Austin and Morris companies, the Mini was originally launched in two versions; the Austin Seven and the Morris Mini-Minor. The Mini would be the most prolific Longbridge product, with over three and a half million produced from Longbridge.

In 1966, the British Motor Corporation and Jaguar merged to form British Motor Holdings (BMH). Two years later a grand alliance of Britain's motor industry was created when the BMC merged with Leyland Motor Corporation to become the British Leyland Motor Corporation (BLMC).

Among the many brands held by the new organisation, two had special future significance.

*Top: Sterling Bomber production at Longbridge during the second world war. **Below:** Veteran Car Parade at Austins Golden Jubilee celebrations in 1955.*

ROVER

Rover cars have been at the heart of Britain's motor industry since 1904. Towards the end of the 19th century, the city of Coventry had become the capital of the British cycle industry. Foremost among many bicycle makers in the city was the Rover Company. Rover had been founded in 1877 as a partnership between John Kemp Starley and William Sutton. While Sutton soon pulled out of the business, Starley was to remain at the helm until his death in 1901.

The Rover Company only entered into production of self-propelled vehicles in 1903, with the first Rover Imperial motorcycle. In the following year, the first Rover car was introduced. Over the next few years, Rover made a wide variety of cars but in 1912 two new cars were introduced to replace all the earlier models - a 3.3 litre 18 hp car and the better-known 2.3 litre 12 hp model.

In 1919 came the Rover Eight, manufactured in a new factory at Tyseley in Birmingham.

The Eight had an air-cooled flat-twin engine, a type of power unit often associated with motorcycles. It was deservedly popular, until eclipsed by the four cylinder Austin Seven. In 1924 Rover brought out a four cylinder Nine, and began to move its products up-market, away from direct competition with the more mass produced Austins and Morrises.

The Nine was replaced by the somewhat undistinguished 10.25 in 1928, which in various forms survived until 1933, and in the same year Rover introduced its first six-cylinder model. The 1928 2-litre had an overhead valve engine and sold for £410 in tourer form. One of these cars, with fabric-covered bodywork, entered the history books by beating the famous Blue Train in a race across France.

At the 1949 Motor Show, Rover showed the new P4 model. This had an all-new body with full width styling in the American style. The range went on to become a much-loved car, best known affectionately as the 'Auntie' Rover. When the P4 range finally bowed out in 1964, more than 130,000 had been built.

Top: Rover 12, 1911-1924.
Below: Rover's 1954 P4 model.

A P4 was the basis for the extraordinary JET 1 of 1950, the world's first gas turbine engine car, inspired by Rover's wartime involvement with the jet engine. This car earned Rover the Dewar trophy for the second time and was driven at speeds over 150mph.

A major step ahead for Rover came with the P5 model of 1958, a large luxury saloon with a 3-litre version of Rover's six-cylinder engine. The 3- and 3.5-litre models became favourites for transport of dignitaries, including Prime Ministers from Harold Wilson to Margaret Thatcher, and HM the Queen.

In 1966 Rover was bought by the Lancashire-based truck maker Leyland, which already owned Standard Triumph. Then in 1968, the Leyland group merged with Britain's largest maker of popular cars, BMC, whose portfolio included Austin, Morris and MG. The next new Rover car was the SD1 of 1976, which like the P6 before it took Car of the Year title.

In 1980 the company worked with the Japanese Honda Company to produce a number of collaborative projects, which included the first Rover small car for many years. The first 200 series of 1984 was also the first front-wheel drive Rover car. A programme of joint development was then started for a new executive car, project XX, which was introduced as the first Rover 800 in 1986.

Originally laid out to produce the 1980 Metro three-door bodyshell, the modern Longbridge body plant was adapted to include production of the shells for the Rover 200 and its Honda Ballade sister model. In 1989, the 'R8' style Rover 200 (five and three-door) and Rover 400 (four door), plus Honda Concerto bodyshells brought further variety and became the most popular model in the Rover brand's history.

Top: *1968 Rover 3500 V8.*
Below: *The 1992 Rover 800 Coupe with H.M. The Queen's Rover P5 outside the gates of Windsor Castle. The P5 (1958-1973) was the first Rover car to be built with unitary bodywork.*

MG

The other key brand is MG. It evolved from Morris Garages, Oxford's leading car dealer, from which the initials were taken and held within an Octagon to form an early example of distinctive branding. In 1924 Cecil Kimber, General Manager of Morris Garages produced a line of special bodied cars on Morris chassis. He took a Morris Cowley chassis and had it fitted with an open two-seater body. This was the first time, these cars were sold as MGs and the famous octagonal badge began to feature in advertisements.

In early 1925 Kimber had a special car built for his own use. This used a much-modified Morris chassis with a special overhead valve version of the side valve Morris engine, and a light racing type body. He entered his car, since known as 'Old Number One' - the first proper MG sports car, in the Land's End Trial at Easter 1925 and won a gold medal. In 1926, the original Bullnose Morris models were replaced by the so-called Flatnose types with a more conventional radiator, and the MGs followed suit.

The most important new model of 1928 was the first MG Midget. This was based on the recently introduced Morris Minor but the bodywork was a fabric-covered two-seater with a pointed tail. The Midget went into full production in March 1929 selling for £175; the success of the new car soon made it clear that it was necessary for MG to move yet again to a bigger factory. At the end of 1929, MG took over part of a factory at Abingdon on Thames a few miles south of Oxford, destined to be MG's home for the next fifty years.

Many more MGs were launched, with the J type of 1932 Kimber established what became the typical MG look: the double humped scuttle and the fold-flat windscreen, the deep elbow cut-outs in the doors, and the petrol tank and spare wheel strapped to the back.

There was a new Midget in 1936, the 1.3-litre TA, replaced just before the war by the improved TB. MG's best pre-war year was 1937 with almost 3,000 cars built. Total production from 1923 to 1939 amounted to some 22,500 cars.

By 1953, and now part of the BMC group, MG had a new general manager, John Thornley. Together with his chief designer Syd Enever, Thornley wanted an all-new sports car to appeal to the vital American market. The 1955 MGA had a new chassis, all enveloping bodywork in contrast to MG's traditional style. This became MG's biggest success story to date with more than 100,000 MGAs made.

The Midget was another favourite with 225,000 produced, but it was the Abingdon-produced MGB that went on the break production records with over 500,000 being made.

Top right: MG's M type Midget 1929-1932.
Above: The MG TF, 1953.
Below: The MGB 1962-1980, MG's biggest selling car with one in every three MGs being a B. Pictured is the 1973 MGB GT V8.

LONGBRIDGE

In 1982 Longbridge revived the fortunes of MG with a sporting version of the parent company's Metro. Over the next few years MG versions of the Maestro and Montego also appeared. MG enthusiasts understandably longed for the day when an all-new MG sports car would return. After the 1992 MG RV8, a re-styled version of the classic MGB roadster, was introduced, a new MG was duly launched at the Geneva Motor Show in March 1995. The MGF went into series production at Longbridge in August 1995, and quickly became enormously successful as the UK's best-selling roadster, year after year.

Longbridge was in the mid 1990s producing the volume of the companies' products for MG, Rover and Mini, supported by the Rover 800 and 600 models at Cowley.

a range of MG ZR, ZS and ZT saloon models and the TF sports car replaced the MGF. By 2002 the range offering had doubled and a high-powered sports coupe was launched as the MG XPower SV. The product and derivative introductions have been impressive, with recent new models including the new Streetwise, CityRover and a 4.6-litre MG ZT 260 V8.

In 2004, Rover's centenary year, the company revised the appearance of its key models with extensive improvements to the 75, 45 and 25, modernising the range appeal. A flagship Rover 75 V8, with a larger prestige grille, was proudly launched at the Geneva Motor Show, with a Longbridge-built 75 Limousine, also featuring the large-grille treatment, the highlight of the Birmingham show.

Similarly, 2004 was MGs 80th anniversary year and the range was updated with a new-look ZR, ZS and ZT, taking the brand similarities of the performance XPower SV.

In 1998 Rover launched the beautifully shaped 75 and followed with the 45 and 25. In 2000, the company returned to independent ownership when the Phoenix Consortium acquired the business from BMW. MG Rover Group was duly formed as a wholly independent UK specialist motor car producer.

The new company set about rapidly introducing many new products, including the acclaimed 75 Tourer estate,

Left: The King and Queen visit Longbridge Aero factory in 1940. Top: MG Rover Group's product portfolio of 2004 from left to right: MG - ZR, TF, ZS, XPOWER SV, ROVER - City Rover, Streetwise, 75 V8, 25, 45, and 75.
Above: MG TF Wheel on facility.
Right: MG Rover Group, Longbridge.

Bird's eye view

What an extraordinary mixture of the old and the new is visible in this remarkable aerial photograph taken in 1967. Dominating the scene is that iconic Birmingham landmark the 500 foot BT tower. All around, beyond the tower, new office blocks and flats are rising. Prime Minister Harold Macmillan famously said at the end of the 1950s that we'd never had it so good: but even he could not have guessed just how relatively prosperous we would be feeling by the mid-1960s. During that decade many of Britain's cities were virtually rebuilt - though not always for the better. With more money around filling in blank spaces in the cityscape now became practical. One of the strangest sights in this view is the astonishing amount of empty space around the Hall of Memory. At the time it sometimes seemed as if the whole of Britain was one huge building site. Vast new roads, motorways, initially with no speed limits, began to cross-cross the country. Architects unfolded futuristic plans: straight lines and smooth concrete would be the watchwords of the space age. Words like 'traditional' and 'classical' were derided as old fashioned and backward looking. The new, no matter how ugly, was to be preferred. Happily not all was replaced. Pride of place on this photo goes to the buildings around Victoria Square: the City Museum and Art Gallery built in the 1880s, the Town Hall completed in the 1860s and the Renaissance style Council House which first opened its doors in 1870s.

Below: The streets at the top of this scene are, from left to right: Great Charles Street, Edmund Street, Colmore Row, Waterloo Street and New Street. Those with sharp eyes will readily make out the Town Hall, Victoria Square, the Council House and the Museum and Art Gallery. In the centre of this 1948 aerial photograph is the unmistakable rotunda of the Hall of Memory. A memorial to those who had died in the first world war, the Hall of Memory was opened in July 1925. On the first day more than 30,000 people filed through the Cornish granite and Portland stone structure, many more thousands would make the solemn pilgrimage over the coming years to pay their respects to the local heroes who had given their lives in what they had believed was 'the war to end wars'. Tragically the first world war was not to be the end of war. And in the second world war which broke out in 1939 it would not just be servicemen and women who gave up their lives. In twenty years technology had moved on making it possible for aircraft to fly from the continent and drop bombs on British cities: not least Birmingham. Bomb sites would remain a feature of the cityscape long after the German surrender in 1945. In 1989 the rectangle in front of the Hall became Centenary Square, flanked by the International Convention Centre and Symphony Hall together with the Repertory Theatre. To the left of the Hall of Memory is another building erected between the wars: the gleaming bulk of Baskerville House.

Right: How many new buildings have been built in our city centre since the end of the second world war? How many old ones have been demolished? And how many new roads, traffic islands and flyovers have appeared? The passage of more than half a century has transformed the centre of Birmingham. This 1948 photograph may look superficially modern, but close examination reveals the full extent of the changes which have occurred to our city over the course of six decades. Railways rather than the car still dominated our lives when this view was captured.

To the left can be seen the open area surrounding St Phillip's Cathedral just below the oblong mass of Snow Hill railway station. At the very bottom of the scene appears New Street station and in the far right Moor Street station Though the roads may not yet be choked with traffic, cars are very much in evidence as witnessed by the very full car park just below

the centre of the picture. Corporation Street cuts across the scene diagonally from bottom left to top right. Along the length of Corporation Street, prior to its junction with Steelhouse Lane, can be made out the Cobden Hotel, Lewis's, the Priory , the Old Square , the Victoria Law Courts and the Methodist Central Hall. Just to the right can be seen the fire station. In the lower right corner can be made out St Martin's Church and the old Bull Ring.

The aerial view, taken from above the city centre, looks across the university and beyond towards where the A38M now takes traffic to link with the M6 motorway. In 1961, such major routes were still in their infancy. The first stretch of motorway, the Preston by-pass, only opened in the late 1950s, but it was obvious from the volume of traffic seen in the centre of this picture that new and faster roads were needed to route through traffic well away from our major towns and cities. At the bottom right of the photograph, Snow Hill Station is flanked by Colmore Row. The station entrance on this side was quite splendid and impressive as it provided access to one of the rail 'cathedrals' of Victorian

Britain. Sadly, much of that façade has now been lost. Snow Hill opened in 1852, though it did not adopt that name until 1858. It was part of the Great Western Railway and initially used Brunel's broad gauge track, before converting to standard gauge in 1861. It was rebuilt 10 years later as passenger traffic increased dramatically, with a further rebuild being required in 1912 when the two platforms were lengthened to 400 yards. Electrification of the line through New Street hastened the end for this station and the last passenger train in operation was seen in 1968, the year after through traffic had stopped. It closed to all users in 1972, but was revitalised and reopened on 2 October 1987.

But for the church, it would be difficult to determine the exact location of this part of the city, taken from a scene captured on film nearly half a century ago. The camera was pointed towards the Bull Ring, once the site of Birmingham's village green and sometimes used as a form of speakers' corner. The right to hold markets in this vicinity was granted over eight centuries ago. Just in front of the clutch of telephone boxes and Midland Red buses near the centre of the photograph, the keen eyed can make out the statue of Nelson. The bronze figure, backed by an anchor and bows of a warship, was the brainchild of Richard Westmacott and set in place in 1809, one of the first such memorials to the hero of Trafalgar, killed just four years earlier. Pride of place in this scene belongs to St Martin's Church. The first one on this site was erected in the 13th century and, following several subsequent rebuilds, the current parish church was designed by JA Chatwin and reconsecrated in the late Victorian era, though its tower and spire date from 1781. After the various regeneration exercises of the latter part of the last century, St Martin's now appears marooned under Nelson's gaze amid the sea of shops and malls as the Rotunda casts its shadow over this historic part of the city.

This aerial view overlooks New Street Station that first saw light of day as a smaller entity in 1851. It took seven years to build and came about partly as a result of the London and Birmingham Railway Company for which father and son, George and Robert Stephenson, acted as engineers. The original station doubled in size when it was developed to straddle Queens Drive in 1880. The huge iron and glass roof, the largest single span construction of its type anywhere in the world at the time, had impressive measurements, even by today's standards. It was 370 yards in length, 70 yards in width and towered 27 yards above the ground. A bridge and a number of subways

linked the platforms to complete a feat of engineering that we rather take for granted from our Victorian predecessors who produced so many stunning examples of inventive workmanship that we have become blasé about their skills. Before the 1921 Railways Act reduced the rail companies to four major players, the London Northwestern Railway and Midland Railway shared the station. After the Act was approved in 1923, New Street was used as the main Birmingham station for the London, Midland and Scottish company. It is now one of four stations serving the city, with Snow Hill, Moor Street and Birmingham International supplying the support.

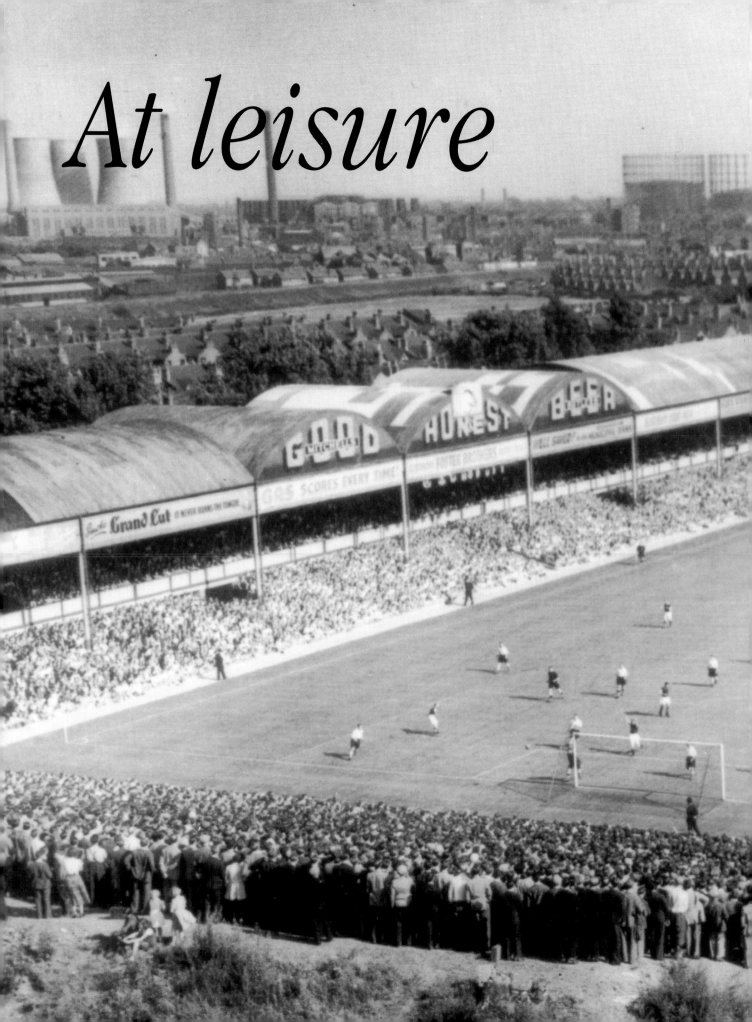

At leisure

Today it costs a fortune to go to a football match. In the 1950s however football was still a poor man's game: poor that is for both players and spectators. Millionaire footballers simply didn't exist in the days when players wages were strictly limited. And buying tickets in advance was not something which occurred to the ordinary football fanatic - it was queue up and pay at the turnstile. Here it's 1952 and Aston Villa are playing Arsenal at Villa Park. This photo really is one for older football fans who can recall the great post-war days with the huge crowds which gathered to watch every spectator sport. There was no such thing as all weather, all covered, all seater stadiums. Stands were exactly that - somewhere to stand. And though covered stands were common enough nearly every football ground in the country seemed to have its bare banking at least one end, covered with nothing more than ash and a little scrubby grass. Given the huge crowds (76,588 people crammed into Villa Park in 1946) and primitive safety conditions its a miracle that there were not disasters every week. Undoubtedly the reason disasters were largely avoided was the discipline of the crowds. Football was very much a family event, as can be seen from the number of children and women here. Football hooliganism was still another decade or more in the future, whilst most young men having been in the forces were used to moving about in large organised groups.

Above: Rowton House was completely revamped in 1993 when it was turned into the Chamberlain Hotel. In 2002 it underwent a further name change to become the Paragon Hotel, a popular place frequented by tourists and locals alike. In 1932 it had a completely different function as a hostel for impoverished menfolk, to whom it first opened its doors in 1903. At the time of this photograph there were many who qualified as men laid low by poverty, because this was during the period of 20th century history when the title 'working class' became a sick joke. These were the depression years when the western world went through an economic slump that lasted for over a decade, from the late 1920s up to the eve of the second world war. The Wall Street crash was a major factor and affected those countries that had strong ties with America. By the mid 1930s, Britain's unemployed numbered 3,000,000 and street riots and hunger marches were features of our lives. The children in Highgate Park could escape from the problems for a while as they enjoyed the swings, roundabouts and seesaws, but many of them would return home to find that bread and vegetables figured largely in their diets. Fresh meat was a luxury afforded to those in work or to the middle classes, though many of the latter struggled as their investments disappeared into thin air.

Left: The idyllic view from 1970 across the pool at Valley Parkway to the undeveloped meadows beyond suggests a rural, peaceful part of Britain with overtones of the 'Darling Buds of May' and could have been from an age when hay was tossed with pitchforks and grandpa was but a lad. There are even little boys in short trousers mooching about, as little boys do, and girls in dresses rather than jeans. Yet, we are in a fairly modern era, just a few miles out of the city centre. At least we can prove from this photograph that the midlands is not exclusively Black Country, but has more than its fair share of delightful, recreational areas. Valley Parkway links the original village of Bournville with Weoley Castle and the lake and a boathouse were built in 1933, largely thanks to the benevolence of the Cadbury family. It was built by workmen drawn from the large numbers of those thrown out of work during the years of the depression. The lake replaced the smaller Rowheath Pool and was initially very popular with model yacht owners who enjoyed racing their toys during one of the crazes of the decade. The project was typical of the Cadbury ethic of

providing work that could also enhance the environment. The Parkway was handed over to the City Council in 1945.

Above: 'Gone fishing', as Bing and Satchmo used to sing, should be the caption for this early wartime scene in Pype Hayes Park, Erdington. This threesome of young lads was in its element, messing about near the water. It mattered little whether the catch was no bigger than a stickleback because the youngsters were having fun and doing what came naturally for any red blooded boy. They got their knees dirty, splashed about and generally scruffed around. At other times they would have fixed a rope to a tree and swung out across the water, whooping like Johnny Weissmuller in some Tarzan movie. Their pockets were stuffed with bits of string, conkers, a rusty penknife and a half eaten toffee wrapped in grubby paper that could be revisited later as such treats were in short supply. A girl, unless she was an out and out tomboy, was not to be tolerated because she had dolls to play with and liked dressing up. Anyway, she cried when she fell over. The Bagot Trustees sold the park and its assorted outbuildings to the City Parks Committee in 1919 for £10,000. The government had requisitioned the playing fields at Castle Bromwich during the first world war for conversion into an aerodrome. Pype Hayes Park acted as a replacement recreation area and was opened to the public on 24 March 1920.

Below: Before every living room acquired a goggle box in the corner, much of our home entertainment and information came via the wireless, as we used to call radio. Toddlers today are dumped in front of 'CBeebies' as they have their breakfast and are usually lifted from the settee, where they spend the next 14 hours, just as the credits for 'Neighbour/estate agent/holiday rep/car dealer from hell' begin to roll. This is known as parenting skill. In 1955, for most children there were two media highlights of the day. 'Listen with mother' was a chance to hear nursery rhymes and stories read aloud over the airwaves before indulging in some potato printing, pastry making or imaginative play with a mum who actually found it fulfilling to be with her child, rather than plonking it in front of the TV or abandoning it at the local nursery. At teatime, 'Children's Hour' was a delightful magazine style of radio show aimed at older children just in from school. Although gardening by radio might make the cynic smirk a little, such items helped promote interest in useful activities. This Children's Hour plot was in King's Heath and these schoolgirls obviously derived great pleasure from tending the plants and nurturing their growth. Today's breed would probably think it was a scene from 'I'm a teen gardening celebrity, get me out of here'.

Right: 'Swing your partner, but not too far. Bring her back with a left hand star.' All the fun of a barn dance was enjoyed on the green at Weoley Hill, Bournville during the celebrations for the Festival of Britain in May 1951. The jamboree was meant to act as a fillip for the general public during the austerity of the postwar years, though may also have had something to do with the Labour government's attempt to revive its flagging popularity. Held on the centenary of the Great Exhibition, not everyone was enamoured by the extravagance and some of the right wing newspapers dubbed the £8,000,000 expenditure as 'Morrison's Folly', criticising Herbert Morrison, the deputy prime minister, as a wasteful spendthrift. The Dome of Discovery and illuminated Skylon in London were costly structures that now seem to be something of a forerunner to the Millennium Dome that caused so much fuss in 2000. However, the dancers seemed to approve. They lived on the estate that was built with a similar character to that of the original Bournville village, though its layout was more informal. Weoley Hill Limited was established in 1914 to provide housing suitable for first time buyers. The homes were equipped with modern electric lighting and had convenient tram links with the city centre. Some 500 houses were built in the interwar years and the district became an attractive suburb with its own church, village hall and post office.

Below: The waste ground of bomb sites became common-place during the 1940s and continued for some time into the following decade until rebuilding work was completed. They were usually a sorry sight, dilapidated places full of bits of brickwork, with weeds growing through the clumps of concrete alongside large puddles. The dreadful damage that resulted from the blitz years had one advantage, though gained at some cost. The cleared areas provided large car parking facilities, at least for those with enough petrol coupons or the wherewithal to purchase a runabout. The bomb sites were also handy for fairgrounds and big tops. Even in the dark days of 1941, Birmingham residents were able to take time out to enjoy the fun of the fair and the excitement of the circus ring. Seen from the Co-op building, this corner of High Street and New Street was a notable feature of the time and, for a while, became known as Big Top Corner. Even in adversity, there was gaiety to be had and Brummies took advantage of those precious moments of light relief. They marvelled at the skills of bareback riders, tightrope walkers and jugglers as they laughed themselves silly at the antics of the clowns. There were hoop-la stalls where the ring never quite fitted over the prize and coconut shies, though replicas replaced the real fruit. We could not get oranges and bananas, never mind anything as exotic as that from a palm tree.

Wartime

Below: Women played a mightily important role in World War II. During the Great War they had taken over many of the traditional male roles by working in engineering plants, driving ambulances and producing munitions. The scale of contributions increased during the 1939-45 conflict. Women between 18 and 50 were expected to play an active role and, by the end of 1941, there was even a form of conscription introduced as they were allocated to specific duties in the workshop and on the land. Volunteer groups had already been well established in the first few months of the last war and women did not limit themselves to any particular age barrier. Grannies operated alongside youngsters fresh out of school, all pulling together to do their bit. Here, c1940 the Grove Lane First Aid Post was established at the baths and this quintet of brave souls showed off some of the rather primitive equipment with which they were supposed to handle emergency situations created by the aftermath of an enemy air raid. These ladies might have looked an ordinary and slightly fragile group, but there was a steely determination about them. It was no role for the faint hearted as they were more likely to have to deal with badly burned and seriously injured victims than any minor ailment that they might have come across in peacetime. This was a mobile unit that went where the action was and the women never knew what dangers lay in front of them on any given occasion that the sirens sounded.

The scene is High Street opposite the News Theatre. The billing outside the cinema speaks for itself: the hope of peace. In September 1938 everyone was hoping for peace rather than war with Germany. Prime Minister Neville Chamberlain had connections with Birmingham going back to 'Radical Joe' Chamberlain and his brand of 'gas and water socialism' of the 1870s. Sadly Birmingham's 'greatest living citizen' had been duped by the Nazi Fuhrer. A decent honest man himself Chamberlain could not believe that any man could be as duplicitous as Hitler would turn out to be. Chamberlain believed that the Germans had been badly done to at the treaty of Versailles which had ended the first world war and that if the Germans' reasonable demands, not least the annexation of the Sudatenland, could be met then a second catastrophic war could be averted. Those who watched the newsreel at the cinema would witness Chamberlain step down from the aircraft which had brought him home for Germany triumphantly waving a piece of paper 'bearing Herr Hitler's signature' which he assured his audience had brought 'peace in our time'. Looking at this billboard today it's hard to forget how great was the tragedy lurking just around the corner, not only for Neville Chamberlain but the whole world. Many sympathisers have argued that Chamberlain was actually an astute politician who cleverly deferred war for twelve moths to enable Britain to better prepare for war. For most however he remains a sad figure who simply got things badly wrong.

Above: They sat in waiting rooms, a lost look upon their faces, waiting for the transport that would whisk them away from the city in which they had lived all their lives. The 1939 evacuation left them bemused as their destiny was seemingly out of their hands. The little ones had no idea what was happening, but at least they had their mothers with them and a comforting thumb to suck. Older children were separated from their parents and despatched to villages and towns that were just dots on a road map to most of them. They carried battered little suitcases that contained what clothing and teddy bears they could manage, plus a postcard already addressed and stamped so that they could keep mum and dad informed about their new homes. Although most of the children were bewildered, the majority were warmly greeted by the families who took them in and soon settled down in their new environment. Even so, however welcoming the surrogate parents might have been, they were not mum and dad. Children were

understandably homesick and their parents missed them terribly. The first few months were known as the 'phoney war', when little in the way of enemy action was observed. Gradually, the youngsters and other evacuees began to trickle back, in ever increasing numbers.

Below left: This is a scene which may bring tears to the eyes of many older readers. At the time it brought tears to the eyes of the many children being sent away to live with strangers. For some youngsters it was the first time they had ever been away from home. There's no doubt however that the evacuation brought far more tears to mothers who had managed to keep up a brave face for the children's' sake, until they were out of sight. The country had declared war on Nazi Germany on 3rd September 1939. Rehearsals for evacuation had however begun as early as 20th July. Messages were sent to local schools on 31st August that evacuations would begin in earnest the following day. Mothers hurriedly packed their children's' bags and suitcases. Gas masks and sandwiches were carefully stowed and each child identified with a luggage label. In the months which followed during the 'Phoney War' many children would find their way back to Birmingham, some running away, others simply being retrieved by parents who had noted that Birmingham had not been obliterated on 4th September 1939 and thought it

would be safe for the remainder of the war. Sadly the premature return of some youngsters would prove to be a fateful choice. Many children had unhappy lives away from their families in the unfamiliar countryside. For others it would be the time of their lives, fresh air, fresh food and new friends with whom they would remain in contact for the rest of their lives

Above: Operation Pied Piper began in earnest in the late summer of 1939. As German tanks rolled across Belgium and Poland and war was declared on Sunday 3 September, desperate parents sought to take advantage of government plans to evacuate children from high risk areas that would be obvious targets in an air raid. The lessons learned from the Spanish Civil War, when squadrons of Nazi planes helped General Franco's forces bomb the population into submission, were taken to heart. Special trains were requisitioned and coaches laid on at bus stations to take children to places of safety. They went to less vulnerable places as Stratford upon Avon and even further afield. The confusion and hubbub as anxious mothers tried to make some sense of what was going on only led to greater distress for the little ones who did not understand why they had to be parted. Tears were abundant as such harrowing scenes were repeated on a daily basis. The children carried small cases and a few sandwiches as they set off on what, for some, would be a nightmare and not an adventure. With luggage labels tied round their necks to identify them, they waved goodbye and wondered what lay ahead. Some were received into families with whom they forged a relationship that would be a lifelong joy, but others went to places where they were treated like skivvies.

Above: One of the most devastating air raids on Birmingham during the second world war took place on 10th April 1941. Though happily spared the firestorm which would be visited on neighbouring Coventry nevertheless Birmingham and its suburbs experienced more than their fair share of suffering and destruction. During the first world war Britain had suffered some bombing: coastal towns such as Scarborough in Yorkshire had been shelled by the German Navy, whilst London had experienced a short-lived campaign of bombing by German Zeppelins. In the intervening years between the end of the first world war in 1918 and the start of the second man's inventiveness had produced fast long distance aircraft which could carry large bomb loads. During the Spanish Civil War in the mid-1930s the Luftwaffe's Condor Legion had demonstrated exactly what such bomber fleets could do to a civilian population: pessimists predicted the deaths of millions in Britain's cities. Though tens of thousands of British civilians would die the death toll was far less than the worst predictions. That things were not far worse was due to a variety of factors: civil defence activities providing early warning of bomber raids, firewatching patrols and the provision of adequate shelters. Hundreds of public shelters were constructed even before the start of the war. And in every garden corrugated iron Anderson shelters covered with earth appeared almost over night. Sadly even with these measures casualties were inevitable, and rescuers daily faced the grisly task of recovering bodies from the wreckage of homes and factories.

Right: When it came, it came with a shattering impact on more than just property. The blitz on Birmingham changed lives forever; lives that managed to get through the carnage, that is. People lost more than their homes. For many, a whole way of life disappeared, never to return. Trust in one's fellow man vanished, because how could you trust anyone who could wreak such havoc on the innocent? When this was happening to us, who cared that the citizens of Hamburg and Dresden would soon be asking the same question? When we returned the fire from the skies with those 1,000 bomber raids we consoled ourselves with the thought that it was just payback. This war confirmed that civilian casualties were inevitable in any conflict and mankind became almost blasé about that dire fact. The scene on John Bright Street, taken on 22 November 1940, shows part of the aftermath of the raid of three nights earlier that was the 50th and heaviest to hit Birmingham during World War II. On this occasion the warning siren sounded at 6.50 pm with the all clear not actioned until 4.29 the following morning. For hour after hour the city was hammered and a pall of smoke hung over Birmingham, blotting out the sun throughout the next day. John Bright Street, named for the 19th century social reformer from Rochdale who served as our MP for over 30 years, was constructed in 1881, cutting across the existing Georgian street pattern that contained some dreadful slum properties.

Edgbaston Street now runs below the new Bull Ring shopping complex and alongside the market area. Just beyond the scene of devastation, pictured on 10 April 1941, the corner of St Martin's Church can be seen, so the photograph was taken from approximately level with a modern entrance to Debenham's. Locals walked along the road, trying to take in the condition to which this part of traditional Birmingham had been reduced. Rubble, fire damaged buildings and shattered plaster-work lay all around them. It must have been quite unsafe as there was still a risk of falling masonry to be considered, but the support services had more urgent matters to which they had to attend. There were obviously flames still smouldering as firefighters continued to pump water across the street. It would have been difficult for anyone on Edgbaston Street that day to appreciate that he was in what had been once a most prestigious part of the city. In medieval times it linked Parsonage Moat with the moated manor house and carried traffic to the Bull Ring market. Only the privileged would have lived here, close to the Lord of the Manor, the church and market, as well as having access to fresh water supplies. An archaeological dig under the indoor market has shown evidence of a 13th century tannery and other discoveries provided a clue that glass, metal and pottery industries flourished in the vicinity.

Right: The wartime photograph illustrates the meaningless nature of carpet bombing. Anything and everything is hit, but what could possibly have been achieved here? This was hardly a place of strategic importance. The sign on the left informs us that cycling is prohibited on the footpath, but we can safely say that its message had been rendered superfluous. The 'road under repair' notice stated the blindingly obvious, but even in times of war the powers that be just had to erect an official notice. Elsewhere, they had been quite swift to take them down. In the early days of the second world war there was great consternation that a German invasion was imminent. As a means of confusing paratroopers who dropped from the sky and tried to make their way across country to some specific destination, many road signs and mileage markers were removed. In some cases, the signpost was realigned so that Much Binding in the Marsh, or whatever place it might have been, now seemed to be to the west instead of the east. Unfortunately, the plan had some drawbacks. Convoys of British lorries, carrying troops or supplies and driven by those not familiar with the district, got lost and their precious cargoes were delayed. We are reliably informed that one set of trucks, with the lead one driven by a Tommy with the thickest Scouse accent ever heard, was sent in completely the wrong direction by a Coleshill farmer because, 'I knew he was a German - couldn't understand a word he said.'

Below: Over 1,500 innocent souls perished in Birmingham during the air raids of World War II, the majority falling in 1940-41 when the Luftwaffe was at its most active before being called away to support Hitler's thrust into Russia. Although official figures are generally vague, it is thought that some 90,000 civilians perished in Britain because of the bombing and the V1 and V2 rocket attacks. The statistics of non combatant death rose dramatically during the last century's various conflicts, as did the attitudes of governments towards them. In the Great War, the slaying of civilians was 'shocking and shameful'. During the Spanish Civil War it was watered down to 'tragic' and by World War II it had become 'inevitable'. In the second half of the century people even spoke of 'acceptable numbers' and, by the time the millennium was reached words that indicated human beings were eradicated completely by the catchall phrase 'collateral damage'. The inhabitants of Medlicott Road did not care for whatever euphemism was being used as they gazed at the house that was once a home on 27 August 1940. As the police constable and warden discussed the situation from a practical standpoint, the local residents commiserated with one another about the destruction of the little mementoes, such as photographs and prized ornaments that were irreplaceable. A cyclist stood and gazed across the garden wall at the scene of senseless waste.

Above: Wherever you looked in the summer of 1940 there was devastation all around. August was the month when the Battle of Britain began in earnest. In London, the Air Ministry calculated that 1,000 German planes invaded the skies over Britain on a daily basis. They targeted airfields, fuel and munitions dumps and power stations in an attempt to soften us up and render our defences so flimsy that they could not withstand an invasion. The RAF flew sortie after sortie and, although its losses were great, thanks to the tenacity and skill of those boys in blue, ably backed by WAAFs on the ground with their radar expertise and plotting boards, the Germans lost three times as many planes as we did. As Churchill said, 'Never in the field of human conflict was so much owed by so many to so few.' The Luftwaffe could not deliver what Hitler wanted and the planned invasion fleet never sailed for Britain. During this period, there was still great damage being inflicted on the ground by the enemy bombing raids that were stepped up after the Battle of Britain was won. It was then that British stoicism was seen at its best. Life went on, perhaps not as usual, but as near to that as we could make it. There was still the shopping to be done and mum, in the foreground, made sure that she was properly turned out with hat and gloves as she made her way past the bedstead that had been blown out of some wrecked bedroom.

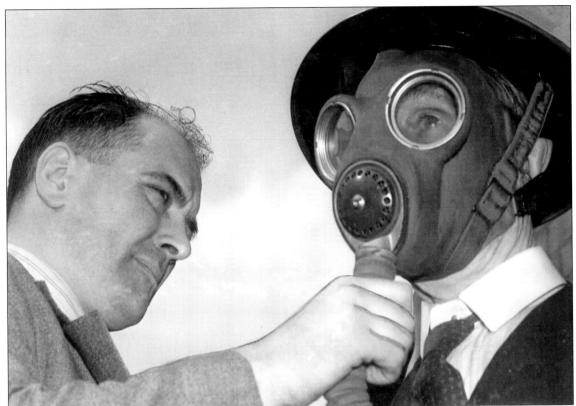

Left: The shopping centre at Martineau Place, sandwiched between Union Street and Bull Street, is named for the family that includes several former Lord Mayors of Birmingham among its ranks. Here seen in his ceremonial robes in a procession from the Council House to the Hippodrome, Wilfrid Martineau (1889-1964) marched with the Pioneer Corps as part of a recruiting drive held during his term of office, 1941-42. His father, Ernest, held the same lofty office (1912-15) and served with distinction in the Great War as Lt Colonel, 6th Battalion Royal Warwickshire (Territorial) Regiment. Ernest's father, Thomas, had also worn the mayoral robes and, to continue the family link, Wilfrid's own youngest son, Alan, held office in 1986-87. The Martineaus had further connections with the city fathers than just their own contributions. They were related by marriage to the Kenrick family, another name that appears on the mayoral role of honour. Joseph Chamberlain, the 'gas and water socialist', is seen by many as the founding father of the Birmingham. He married Harriet Kenrick in 1861 and, so it can be seen that the guiding hand on Birmingham's municipal controls has, at times, been interwoven with long standing family ties. When Wilfrid Martineau marched alongside the troops he was giving his support to the need to bolster numbers actively engaged in the war effort. In December 1941, the upper age limit for conscription was raised to 50, so acute was the manpower situation.

Above: As we reached the final years of the 1930s it was becoming apparent that the threat of war across Europe was no longer an idle one. Mr Chamberlain, our very own former Lord Mayor, became prime minister in 1937 and made three visits to Germany in the following September in a forlorn attempt at appeasing Hitler's territorial ambitions. But, it was all to no avail and the tanks rolled into Czechoslovakia. On the home front, Britain realised that war was almost inevitable. Belatedly, plans for the defence of the realm were formulated and attention given, for the first time ever, to the fate of the civilian population when hostilities broke out. The experience of men in the trenches in the Great War led many to believe that chemical warfare was a real threat. This time, with lessons learned from the Spanish Civil War, the country knew that aerial bombardment would be something with which we would have to reckon. That those bombs might contain poisonous gases was something we could not ignore, so civil defence groups quickly organised practices and drills in the event of an onslaught by the enemy. Gas masks were issued, with particular emphasis to those living in heavily populated and industrial areas, the probable focus of attack. Here, preparations were made for an instructors' course at Birmingham's new Civil Defence Technical Training School. Mr N Cartwright helped adjust the appliance that he hoped Jack Henderson would never have to use.

In the immediate post war years when folk should at last have been feeling once more safe in their beds the reverse was sadly true. We may have had the Bomb but thanks to the work of communist spies so now did the Russians. Euphoria at the German defeat was soon followed by a paranoid fear of Reds under the beds, and the prospect of a global nuclear war far worse than anything which had been experienced in the years of the second world war. This photo of a Food Flying Squad was taken on 22nd November 1953 in the Civic Centre car park near Cambridge Street. 'Operation Aspirin' was one of a series of Civil Defence exercises providing practice for a civil emergency. Almost on her knees is Mrs JH Bowden of

the Women's Voluntary Service cooking apple tarts in the oven of the Bluff Cooker; basting meat is Mr RA Bashford area manager of Civic restaurants and a Civil Defence Emergency Instructor. Stood next to Mr Bashford are Mrs Hackett and Mrs Rhodes, two more keen WVS members. The Food Flying Squad consisted of four mobile canteen vans a water tanker and two stores vans. Crewed by WVS volunteers the electric blue vans were part of a emergency convoy of 16 vehicles for Birmingham under the control of the Ministry of Food; in theory they were allegedly capable of providing 8,000 meals in a crisis. Though always ready to help, many volunteers were secretly sceptical of their value in the event of a nuclear attack.

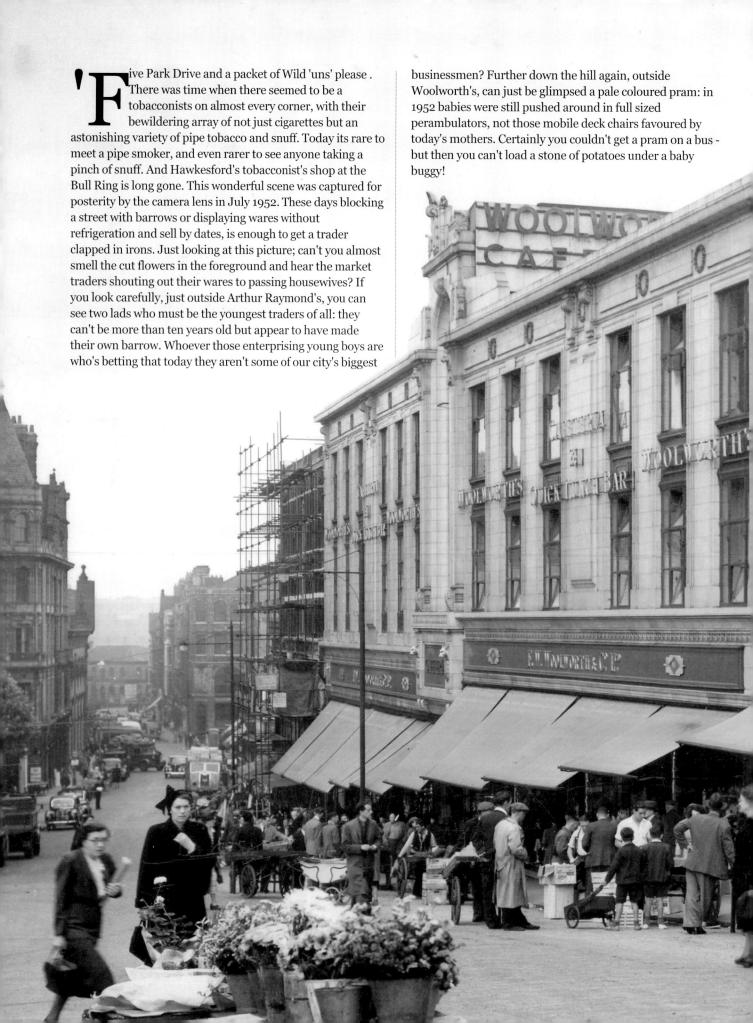

'Five Park Drive and a packet of Wild 'uns' please . There was time when there seemed to be a tobacconists on almost every corner, with their bewildering array of not just cigarettes but an astonishing variety of pipe tobacco and snuff. Today its rare to meet a pipe smoker, and even rarer to see anyone taking a pinch of snuff. And Hawkesford's tobacconist's shop at the Bull Ring is long gone. This wonderful scene was captured for posterity by the camera lens in July 1952. These days blocking a street with barrows or displaying wares without refrigeration and sell by dates, is enough to get a trader clapped in irons. Just looking at this picture; can't you almost smell the cut flowers in the foreground and hear the market traders shouting out their wares to passing housewives? If you look carefully, just outside Arthur Raymond's, you can see two lads who must be the youngest traders of all: they can't be more than ten years old but appear to have made their own barrow. Whoever those enterprising young boys are who's betting that today they aren't some of our city's biggest businessmen? Further down the hill again, outside Woolworth's, can just be glimpsed a pale coloured pram: in 1952 babies were still pushed around in full sized perambulators, not those mobile deck chairs favoured by today's mothers. Certainly you couldn't get a pram on a bus - but then you can't load a stone of potatoes under a baby buggy!

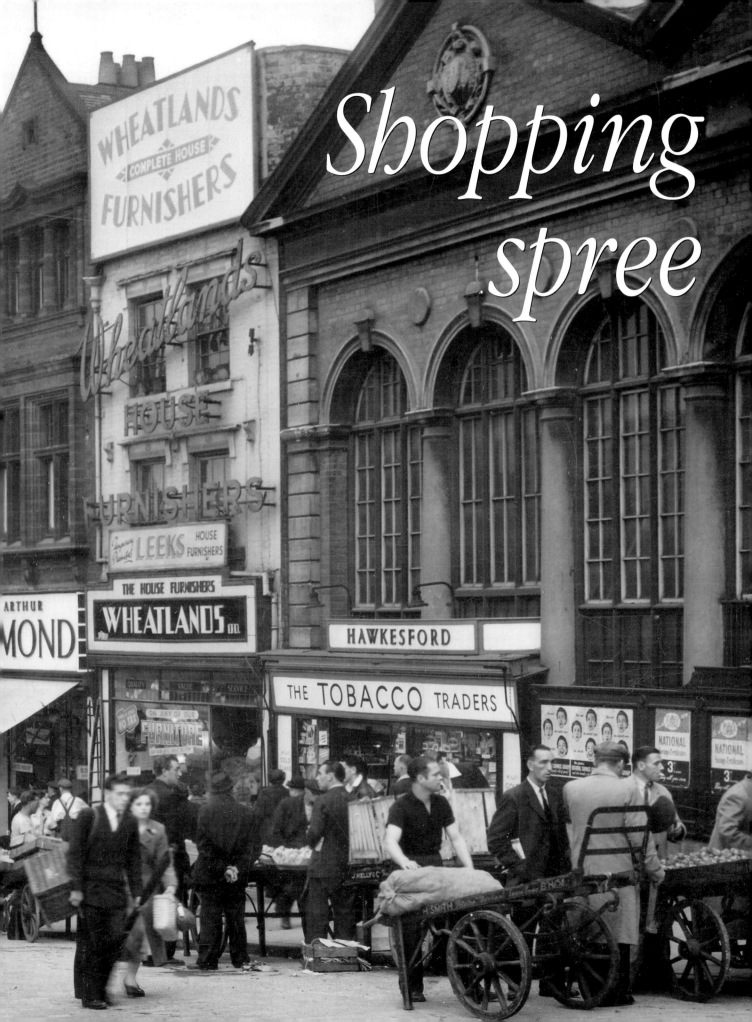

Shopping spree

The High Street in the summer of 1952 presents an image of a far quieter world than the one we now inhabit. Back then there were no huge shopping centres, instead each shop was an individual business. On the far right is Stylo where we went to buy our shoes. Paul Taylor Ltd was where we went to buy our bedding, carpets and lino, as had our fathers and their fathers before them - the household goods firm had been in business in Birmingham since the 1840s. Next door to Taylors is the Board Inn, handy for Dewhirst's butchers with its facade dominated with its huge advert for Hurrell's Dairyfeed bacon, supplies of which appear to just being

delivered. Perhaps the greatest change to be found in modern streets is not the shops but street lighting. Outside Paul Taylor's shop is one of the most evocative symbols of yesteryear: a gas lamp. For children brought up before the 1960s the gas lamp at the end of the street was the centre of their lives. In summer the gas lamp provided the wicket for our games of street cricket, in winter a goalpost for football. In the absence of adventure playgrounds it could be a swing and a trapeze. The cast iron pillars were robust enough to take any amount of rough treatment. The glass was a different matter, though surprisingly few panes got broken. Perhaps the soft light cast by gas somehow made people gentler than does today's harsher sodium lighting.

Above: There always was a crush of folk in this part of Birmingham as they weaved their way in and out of the stalls and roadside barrows. Although the sun shone brightly, the warm clothing sported by shoppers in the Bull Ring open air market suggested that this was winter in 1954. Notice that it is only the younger generation of men and lads who are going around bareheaded. Those of more mature years favoured trilbies, homburgs and flat caps, dependent upon their social standing. The cut flowers and potted plants seem to have attracted some interest. No doubt their perfume helped to mask the odours coming from the fish stores opposite. Half a century ago, fish was an important Friday commodity among the Catholic population as it was on that day that they abstained from the eating of meat. This religious custom, born partly from the notion of penance and partly as a way of respecting the fish as an ancient symbol of Christianity, was often copied by those who did not subscribe to the same beliefs. Friday was often a fish day for both the heathen and the devout. Even in our Godless 21st century homes, many of us still use the local 'chippy' at the end of the working week, though the habit is now down to convenience rather than any firmly held conviction.

Below: Seen in the 1950s, Corporation Street was then, as now, one of the city's main shopping areas. Looking down the hill past Fore Street on the right and towards the junction with New Street at the bottom of the hill, many of these fine buildings are happily still with us. Their ground floor designs and businesses may have changed, but there are still fine examples of our forefathers' architecture to be enjoyed. Even the handsome clock ticks away as merrily as it ever did, though a cosmetics company now trades beneath its pawnbroker symbol. The shop with the awning to the left of the clock is now a hairdresser's, while Roberts and Mappin and Webb trade from premises on either side of the clock. Swears and Wells has become Jade and the shop on the far right is part of the H Samuel chain. This site had been home to the well patronised Midland Educational Company, a bookshop that specialised in schoolbooks. Latin primers, copies of Shakespearean plays and geometry tomes, with the mysteries of Pythagoras, alternate angles and the formula of $2n - 4$ explained as a means of calculating the number of degrees in a polygon, were all here to educate or confuse inky fingered pupils. The shop faced across Corporation Street, looking down Union Street.

Lewis's at the junction of Corporation Street and Bull Street closed in 1991, but here in the 1950s the once mighty store is still a magnet for Birmingham's shoppers. On the right, opposite Lewis's, is another much visited store, Dolcis. By the 1950s the post war economic boom was making itself felt everywhere, not just in the takings in shops but on the roads. The volume of cars had begun to increase remarkably, as the three lanes of vehicles queuing at the traffic lights between two lines of parked cars vividly illustrates. The volume of traffic made necessary the introduction of the one way system so hated by motorists, though these motorists had yet to experience the twin curse of the double yellow line and the traffic warden. Perhaps the most unfamiliar piece of street furniture to younger eyes can be found in the lower right hand corner of the scene. Youngsters asked to identify that odd looking bollard will be mystified. It is of course a police telephone. In the days before mobile phones and handheld radio sets policemen who wanted to get in touch with the police station had to phone home. Opening the door in the cast iron box would reveal a dedicated telephone for the police officer to use. Conversely if the sergeant back at the station wanted to get hold of the bobby of the beat he could ring the box causing an orange light in the lantern atop it to flash on and off.

Standing outside FW Woolworth's, originator of the five and ten cent store, in 1938 provided a view up Spiceal Street beyond the old Market Hall on the left and Nelson's statue in the centre, up the hill towards the bottom end of New Street and High Street. The 271 foot high Rotunda has dominated the far end of this scene since 1965, but before the war and for most of the next two decades that followed this was a busy shopping area where barrow loads of produce were on sale at the kerbside. The Bull Ring markets, behind the camera, also were in full swing, doing a roaring trade. On the left, a delivery boy pedalled his tricycle that had a front basket laden with goods. People used to measure the popularity of songs of the day by the number of times these lads would whistle them as they went about their work. 'A nice cup of tea' could have been both on his lips and in his thoughts as he pumped his legs hard in an effort to shift his heavy load up the slope. A bicycle propped against the wall of the grounds of St Martin's church is a reminder that we did once live in an age when people respected one another's property. It would not last five minutes today unless it was padlocked and chained to an immovable object. Virtually everything has now gone from this spot, with all the buildings consigned to the history books. Even the church railings have disappeared and Spiceal Street was expunged from the local A to Z many moons ago.

Happily this handsome edifice escaped the major architectural influences of the mid 20th century, namely the wartime blitz and the ideas of modern builders and planners. It still stands as an example of the way in which noble structures should be created. It was caressed into life rather than thrown together in a burst of pre cast concrete fusing with steel and glass. There is an elegance and majesty about this corner of New Street and Corporation Street that thumbs its nose at the brash youth of buildings that offer little to the eye but an awful lot to the wallet. Pictured in 1964, we were well into the swinging 60s when young people were starting to set the agenda. Young men and women no longer aspired to be like good old mum and dad. They started to dress differently from their parents. Men actually owned more than one suit that did for church, weddings and funerals. They even stopped putting Brylcreem on their hair and washed it more than once a week as, horror of horrors, their locks crept down the forehead and over the collar. Women started to look for dresses that did not have flowery prints and used words like 'fab' and 'groovy' that, to older ears', were incomprehensible. Looking up from Queen's Corner, we can see the Birmingham Post offices and the Kardomah Café, with its fine arts and crafts interior next to Austin Reed on the corner of Cannon Street. Jane Norman occupies the main corner nowadays, with a number of other illustrious clothes shops beyond.

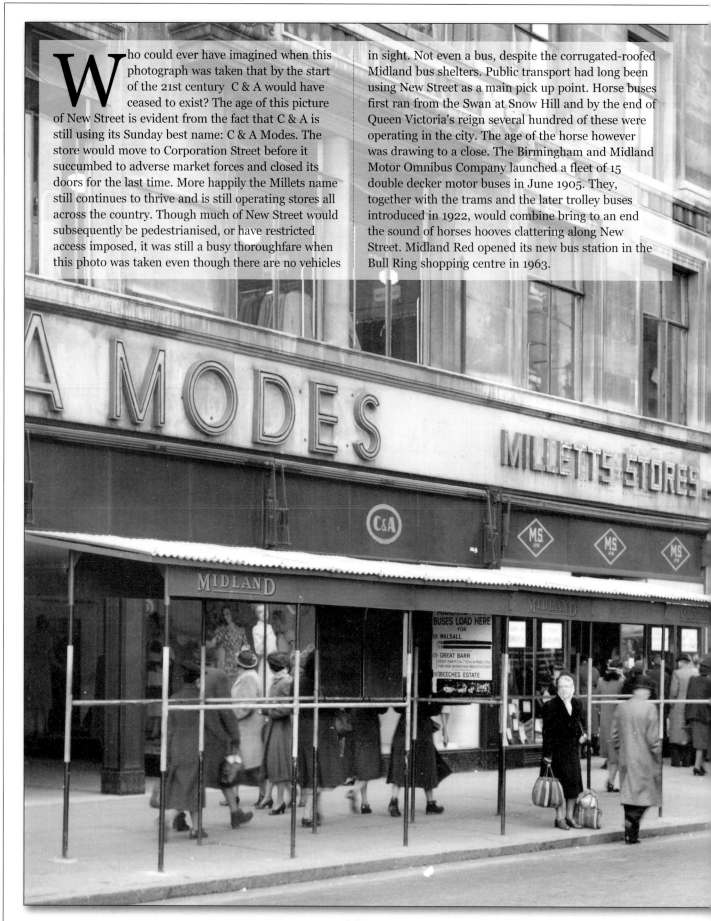

Who could ever have imagined when this photograph was taken that by the start of the 21st century C & A would have ceased to exist? The age of this picture of New Street is evident from the fact that C & A is still using its Sunday best name: C & A Modes. The store would move to Corporation Street before it succumbed to adverse market forces and closed its doors for the last time. More happily the Millets name still continues to thrive and is still operating stores all across the country. Though much of New Street would subsequently be pedestrianised, or have restricted access imposed, it was still a busy thoroughfare when this photo was taken even though there are no vehicles in sight. Not even a bus, despite the corrugated-roofed Midland bus shelters. Public transport had long been using New Street as a main pick up point. Horse buses first ran from the Swan at Snow Hill and by the end of Queen Victoria's reign several hundred of these were operating in the city. The age of the horse however was drawing to a close. The Birmingham and Midland Motor Omnibus Company launched a fleet of 15 double decker motor buses in June 1905. They, together with the trams and the later trolley buses introduced in 1922, would combine bring to an end the sound of horses hooves clattering along New Street. Midland Red opened its new bus station in the Bull Ring shopping centre in 1963.

Above: Even in late 1952 there was still plenty of evidence of the havoc wreaked during the war years when the German Luftwaffe left its explosive calling card night after night. Shattered and gutted buildings waited for demolition and scaffolding propped up those that might be repaired or rebuilt. In the shadow of these reminders of those terrible days, shoppers went about their normal business. Rationing was still with us, but many restrictions had been relaxed as goods and raw materials became more readily available. The main problem, however, was that the average pay packet did not stretch too far and we battled against the drabness and austerity of those early postwar years wondering just who had done best out of winning the war. Success against the enemy had not brought prosperity. Some of the goods on the stalls and barrows in the open market brought a gleam to the eye, however. The pile of boxes of dates tell us that Christmas could have not been too far away, so that was something to look forward to. The Bull Ring would eventually see two major phases of redevelopment. Some wanted to keep the old Market Hall and reroof it, while others favoured retention of the open market. The traditional heart here was destroyed when the Park Street multi storey car park and St Martin's House were built. Even these did not last, being demolished at the end of the last century when the new era of regeneration started to take shape.

Although the concrete awning has now been reduced, this corner of High Street, with the lower end of Bull Street off to the left, is still recognisable several decades after the photograph was taken. The shop on the far left belonged to Evans, still a major name on many other cities' high streets. There is now a significant difference in the way in which it advertises its products as the description 'the outsize shop' is not one that the clothier pushes any more. That is hardly surprising and it is quite remarkable that it ever thought that ladies of indeterminate measurements would appreciate such a term as being appropriate. Bluestar clothes store now trades from these premises. Next door was home to Burton's, 'the tailor of taste', the

company founded by Montague Burton. His chain of stores advanced rapidly from humble beginnings at the start of the last century. He acquired a huge factory in Leeds in 1925, employing 10,000 workers and was said to opening a new shop every month in the 20s and 30s. By World War II he was clothing a quarter of the male population. On demob from the war, men were kitted out with a full set of clothes ready for civvy street. This was known as getting the 'full Monty' and nothing to do with a movie about male strippers. The loading bay for Martineau Place is now just beyond this shop. The opposite corner property at the right hand junction with Dale End has been demolished and Adams children's wear trades from the replacement store.

Working life

Below: Air supremacy was of paramount importance during the war as we strove to protect our little islands from assaults by Hermann Goering's Luftwaffe and began to hit back with our own raids on enemy territory. Castle Bromwich Aeroplane Factory was built in 1938 in anticipation of the declaration of war. Initially, it began by making frames, but soon was established as one of the main production lines in the country in this field. Some 11,000 Spitfire fighter planes and 300 Lancaster bombers were built as a major contribution to the war effort. Women carried out a lot of the work. Here, in 1943, a group was involved in hand stitching fabric to rudders. In other parts of the factory women operated machinery, welded and generally turned their hands to jobs more traditionally associated with the men who had left to join the armed forces. The country turned to its women in the Great War, but most lost their jobs when the men returned from the front and they were forced to return to employment in domestic service or take up office work. Professions such as nursing and teaching were largely restricted to the unmarried. During World War II, the call went out once more for them to head for the factory floor. The hours were long and some had to leave home to move to where the work lay.

There seem to be a lot of gaffers in this photograph and not too many indians actually carrying out any work. Such is the nature of the British workforce and, although we continually knock it, this seems to be the way of our working world. Repairs at New Street Station have, in more recent times, been necessitated on two main occasions. The first came after the war, when damage caused in the blitz took over two years to put right. Rebuilding work began in earnest in October 1945, but was not completed until just after the railways were nationalised at the start of 1948. This was when the 'big four', established in 1923, were amalgamated under one banner as British Railways. The LMS, LNER, SR and 'God's Wonderful Railway', the GWR, came under the control of the state when the 1947 Transport Bill was approved in the House of Commons. In truth, they had not been truly run as individual companies since the start of the war as the government had stepped in at the start of the hostilities in order to co-ordinate the transport network. Although largely undamaged by enemy action, the rail network had become run down because of the obvious lack of investment. Further major changes came to New Street in the Beeching era and the station and lines were modified from 27 April 1964 to meet the needs of electrification.

Left: In just a few years' time these men would be urged to dig for victory as they turned playing fields into allotments and lawns into vegetable patches. On 17 August 1936, the council workmen were shovelling hard as they made alterations to the temporary traffic island at the junction of Bull Street and Corporation Street. Quite a little knot of spectators had gathered outside Lewis's store to watch the work in progress. There must be something in the English character that encourages us to hang around observing such a mundane activity, but we all do it. In some cases, perhaps the men had an excuse to stand on the street corner. 'It is all right, love, you go into the store while I wait out here for you', was often on the lips of hubbies too bored to want to continue the shopping expedition. At least the workmen offered some form of entertainment to help them endure the next half an hour. The traffic lights on the right were still a novelty in many places. Electrically operated ones only made their mark on our major cities at the start of the 1930s. The middle of the decade brought other road safety measures, such as driving tests, Percy Shaw's cats' eyes and Mr Hore-Belisha's famous beacon and its crossing.

Below: Jumbles of parcels, sacks full of letters, trolleys and various oddments littered the platform on New Street Station on New Year's Day, 1947. Above them, the metal spars and scaffolding provided a canopy that was not the result of some over zealous revelry from the night before, but a legacy of enemy action during the war. Reconstruction work on the roof and bridge was under way in an effort to return the station to its former glory. It had been hit not just once, but no fewer than half a dozen times during the years when Birmingham winced and ducked as the sound of explosions ripped through he city, night after night in the first period of the war. All around the station lay a mass of tangled metal that included parts of the platforms, signal boxes and tunnels. Razor sharp shards of glass lay everywhere. The imposing girder roof had been designed by EA Cowper and measured a mighty 840 feet by 210 feet, a true testament to the skill of Victorian engineers. The 1,050 tons of cast and wrought iron supported an immense glassed roof that itself weighed some 115 tons. The station opened on 1 June 1851 and was a part of one of the major factors that changed the lives of the British for evermore as the railways provided access to the length and breadth of the country.

Above: The crane behind the temporary hoarding became a familiar feature in Birmingham during the latter part of the 20th century. First of all we had the rebuilding exercise of the immediate postwar years as bomb damaged properties were taken down and sites cleared to make way for replacements to be erected. In recent years there has been the regeneration phase that has further remodelled the city centre and created the new Bull Ring complex. In between, there was the first shopping regeneration phase of the 1960s, from which time this photograph dates. The camera was located close to where one of Waterstone's outlets can now be found, with the Rotunda and Bull Ring further away to the right. The police in charge of the traffic flow down High Street seem to be too high powered for such a humble duty. We have a sergeant and, presumably from his peaked cap and coat, an even more senior officer in attendance. The latter appears to be directing the limousine towards a particular spot. Perhaps the car contained some VIP or important official, though what would be the purpose of the visit is hard to imagine. Our city has had more than its share of upheaval over the years, so let us hope that no-one has another redevelopment scheme up his sleeve. Brummies on High Street now want to shop until they drop without any more bright wheezes, thank you very much.

Top right: Even the adults found the children's entertainment a hoot. That chap in the three piece suit at the back thought it hilarious, though a poor little soul on the front row seems to have needed comforting. Perhaps she was startled by some of the antics taking place in front of her. Few readers will have failed to guess that the children were watching a Punch and Judy show. The traditional fun of strings of sausages, plodding policemen, Mr Punch bashing his missus and then getting his comeuppance has now become 'something to be banned' by outraged groups who think that such sights will inspire kiddies to turn into evil monsters. Perhaps 'outrageous groups' would be a better description. We do not give youngsters enough credit because, even at an early age, they can easily distinguish fact from fiction. The photograph was taken on Ladies' Day, c1960, at King's Heath Cricket Club. Women were not permitted to be members, though families were welcomed as guests, and the men organised special ladies' days. The club was founded in 1868 and is the oldest existing sports club in the district. A number of former members graduated through the ranks to play at county level. The clubhouse and grounds at 247 Alcester Road South were purchased in 1927 and have been extended in recent years, with squash facilities now covering where Mr Punch once entertained.

Right: The women working in the laundry at Winson Green Prison contributed to the efficiency of the establishment as costs were kept down by having an in-house set up, rather than using outside agencies. The jail was built in the Pentonville style and opened its first cell door on 17 October 1849, rapidly closing it again behind the first miscreant to be confined there. Birmingham's first prison was a modest affair on Peck Lane where New Street Station now stands. As Birmingham's population expanded, so did the number of criminals and the new one was established on Birmingham Heath. It was

designed by DR Hall and described in the local press as ' a brightness compared with some of the surrounding houses'. That may have been true, as the homes in the vicinity were little better than hovels. Government inspectors, though, were far from impressed with the treatment meted out to the inmates. An 1854 report referred to 'a tenth rate shocker, with manacles, straitjackets and thrashings in the name of justice'. Despite the damning comments, Winson Green continued its work and the original 336 cells were increased to 612 in 1885. It was one of Britain's 'hanging prisons' and 33 men and 1 woman went to the gallows there during the last century. The 20 year old Oswald Grey, executed on 20 November 1962 for the murder of Thomas Bates in Edgbaston, was the last one to be despatched in such a way. In the summer of 1964, the prison was in the headlines again when train robber Charlie Wilson escaped. He was recaptured in Canada three and a half years later.

Day's shoe shop at 115 New Street was more than just an ordinary supplier of footwear. Its surroundings suggested that it was a cut above the rest, with its art deco design and distinctive building situated on the corner of Lower Temple Street. Day's was a prominent landmark on the retail front for many years and was regarded by successive generations as the shop for shoes. It prided itself on only selling the very best and its products were stylish, if rather exclusive and expensive. Quality does not come cheap, as the woman on the right was discovering as she carefully checked her purse in this busy scene from c1950. Fashion conscious women in the early postwar years were happy to return to clothing that was feminine and not utilitarian. They had struggled in the war years, making do and mending as the government slogans recommended, and were happy to embrace the greater freedom granted them as clothing rationing began to be relaxed. No more gravy browning for the legs as stockings became available once again. Hemlines dropped and the 'A look' was in. A girl, of course, just had to have the right shoes to complete the ensemble and there was no better outlet than Day's. The shop still stands, but is now a Starbuck's coffee house.

Forge to flightpath

Today in the 21st century Smiths Aerospace Components - Tyseley Ltd, based in Redfern Road, Tyseley is synonymous with cutting edge aviation technology. Smiths Aerospace as a whole, with 11,000 staff and an annual turnover of $1.8 billion, is a leading global provider of innovative solutions to builders and operators of military and civil aircraft and engines from fighters and transport aircraft to large civil, regional and business jets.

Within the Smith 'family', Smiths Aerospace Components businesses are world leaders in gas turbine engine components, supplying every major engine programme across the world - not least the frame for Thrust 2 which broke the land speed record, as well as, more surprisingly, all the cycle frames for the Tour de France winners throughout the 1970s.

Locally the business can trace its roots back to 1841 when one John Reynolds, a nail maker, established himself in Morville Street, Ladywood.

By 1870 John Reynolds had become John Reynolds & Sons of the Chunk, Crown and Phoenix Nail Works in Newton Row, Birmingham.

That early business would in turn give rise in 1898 to the Crown Nail Works and, more importantly to our story, to the Patent Butted Tube company founded by Alfred Reynolds.

It was in 1916 that the company entered the aerospace business, supplying tubes for aircraft manufacture, as well as in 10ft 6 in lengths for making lances for Russian Cavalry. The Patent Butted Tube company would trade under that name until 1923. By now located at the Hay Hall Works in Tyseley the company would change its name to the Reynolds Tube Company.

By 1977, still based at Hay Hall Works, the business had become TI Reynolds and given birth to three subsidiaries: TI Reynolds 531, TI Reynolds Rings and TI Hollow Extrusions.

Reynolds Rings Ltd would become part of the Smiths Group in 2000 before altering its name in 2004 to Smiths Aerospace Components - Tyseley Ltd.

Customers today include Rolls Royce, GE, Pratt & Whitney, Snecma and MTU - all names which were still to achieve prominence when John Reynolds first set up his nail making business in Birmingham back in 1841.

*Top: Reynolds Wings for Victory wartime poster. **Far left:** The production of the first Flash Butt welded ring made at Tyseley for Rolls-Royce in 1952. **Left:** A display of Smiths Aerospace engine components, 2004.*

The secret's in the mail

Based on the Woodgate Business Park, Kettles Wood Drive the Welconstruct Distribution company is today part of the Welconstruct Group, an organisation with some 200 employees and an annual turnover of £35 million.

The company has been designing, selling and installing equipment in the workplace since the end of the Second World War. Selling through its 'Welconstruct in the Workplace' catalogue the firm offers its customers storage equipment, packaging, safety and security equipment, workstations, handling equipment, furniture, environmental and waste equipment and cloakroom furniture and fittings.

Above: Edgar Albert Welch.
Right: The Welconstruct Company's first set of full year accounts, 1946.

'Welconstruct in Education' offers a wide range of products for the classroom, laboratory, workshop, library, staff room, gym, canteen and playground, combined with products for use by the site manager or caretaker such as cleaning, storage and handling products.

For the healthcare sector 'Welconstruct in Health' features sections covering not only healthcare but also administration and premises facilities as well as a range of specialist products designed for use in many areas throughout hospitals including wards, theatres and sterile services.

In the 21st century, Welconstruct is a small medium-sized firm, with some interesting concepts of running a business and with a steady growth and evolution over some 83 years. How did the story begin?

The company began a change of pattern and growth immediately following the end of the Second World War, but the history of the company began much earlier than that.

Edgar Albert Welch was born in 1882. According to legend Edgar ran away from home three times before he was 14. On the third occasion he set himself up as a plumber with a trade card in the window of his digs. Though not a very good plumber he did have the knack of being able to improvise using any materials lying around.

Nicknamed 'Pat' and never known as 'Edgar' or 'Albert', E.A.Welch wandered the Home Counties and South Wales before fetching up in Birmingham. In 1918, being unfit for military service because of his chronic asthma, he was working as an electrician at Best and Lloyds in Wattville

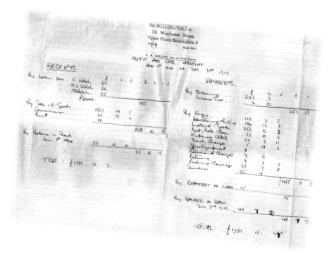

Road, Handsworth. Faced with the problem of fixing switchgear to the round structural cast-iron pillars of the factory he had the idea of getting 12 inch lengths of slotted angle cast in the works foundry. These could be bolted on to each other round the pillars and attached to form a framework. So, Slotted Steel was born. It was with this Slotted Steel that Mr Comino made racks and stands for his printing company, where he evolved the idea of using unequal slotted angles to enable cross-bracing to happen. Comino then printed his own literature about it and Dexion was born as a Company and as a world-wide trade - and indeed - generic name.

In 1918, E.A.Welch also met Elsie Grimmitt on the Handsworth tram and they married. As a socialist and as a non-combatant in the 1914-18 war, E.A.Welch was not immediately popular with the Grimmitt family. In the following year, the Welches' twin son and daughter were born; Cleg eventually to follow a distinguished military career and Mary to become highly respected in Personnel Management circles, a director of the M.E.B. and a J.P. Soon afterwards E. A. Welch left Best and Lloyds and set up a business making electrical fires. In those days each town had its own Electrical Lights Company; some were entirely private, but most belonged to the local Town Council; both the fires and the slotted steel were sold to electricity companies by advertising with circulars. The slotted steel made an excellent fitting for electrical advertising signs but the work also led to using the material for racks of various types that could be fitted with slotted steel shelving.

In November 1922 E.A.Welch had an exhibition at the Agricultural Trade Hall in Islington. Everything on

E.A.W.'s stand was made of slotted steel: the stand, the tables, the shelving, even the chair.

In Islington E.A.Welch met ex-Squadron Leader Donald Finer of Constructors Ltd. As a result they agreed to do business together making shelves from steel - despite the fact that when Donald Finer sat on E A Welch's steel chair it collapsed!

From 1922-1926 slotted steel products were made by E.A.Welch at a works in Mary Anne Street in Hockley under the name Welco Patents, with Constructors Ltd as the selling agents. A 1924 catalogue featuring a new name, Welconstruct, the result of the Welco/Constructors Ltd collaboration, would feature a remarkable number of items and ideas which would be the basis of many of today's storage systems and sales techniques.

During the mid 1920s however, disagreements occurred and by 1927, Constructors Ltd began producing its own materials. Both parties agreed not to use the Welconstruct name in future. E.A.Welch continued manufacturing and his slotted steel shelving continued to be produced by the company until the 1980s. The Welconstruct name was to be resurrected in 1945 when the Welches broke their pledge.

Shelving was not E.A.Welch's only product in this period: in 1927 his second son, Patrick, was born.

Four years later in 1931, E. A. Welch had a factory for his company - Allied Products and Slotted Steel Ltd - at 176,

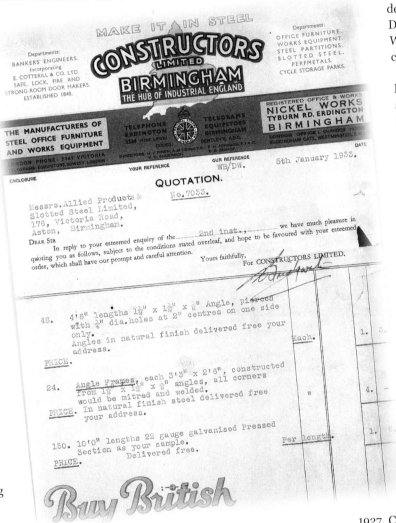

Above: A quotation from Constructors Limited to Allied Products & Slotted Steel Ltd in 1933.

Victoria Road, Aston. The Welch family lived next door in what is now a garage.

Life was not easy. E.A.Welch suffered from asthma and bronchitis every winter which meant that he was virtually always out of action during the winter. This meant he had to take on a series of partners, though none of them lasted: E.A.Welch was not good at building on his successes, not least because in addition to his breathing problems he also suffered from the fact that his thinking and his methods differed from the norm.

Despite such difficulties some fairly considerable jobs were carried out. E.A.Welch's younger son would recall sitting in the cockpit of a Bristol transport plane at Filton whilst his father's company was putting up a series of stores there. Halfords and all the Walpamur (Crown Wallpapers) depots throughout the country were fitted out with shelving. At the same time E.A.Welch designed and made the standard angle iron steel swing which was eventually copied and turned out in many thousands by other people.

During the war years Welconstruct equipment was made by Benfords Ltd of Warwick.

Towards the end of the war, Welconstruct took on a series of primitive workshops around Balsall Heath and made knocked-down, unpainted tool lockers out of such parcels of off-cut steel which could be obtained without an 'M' form (the method of rationing steel). The lockers were all advertised by circulars - the later Welconstruct direct mailing enterprise was in effect born with envelopes being addressed at the rate of 1d for a dozen by the Welch children.

E.A.Welch's younger son's school days ended in August 1945 at the close of the war. Having failed his medical for the armed forces and failed to get a university place Pat now started working full time for the business at a wage of 30 shillings (£1.50) a week; an event which would lead to his remaining in the same job for 57 years.

In the early months of 1945, E.A. Welch had already sold the know-how of making slotted shelving to a firm which eventually became Metalrax, for £1,000.

Welconstruct now rented a tiny office in Upper Priory and found a firm, C.A. Fry Ltd of New Cross, which agreed to make bins and work pans for it. Welconstruct started circularising, and a few desultory orders rolled in. Turnover from August 1945 - July 1946 was just £1,000 of which £250 was the last payment from Metalrax. By contrast the annual turnover of Constructors Ltd with whom E.A.Welch had split in the 1920s was now £1 million.

More money making ideas were clearly needed. Before the war the Welch family had started to build a double storey slotted steel garage at their home in Broad Road, Acocks Green. They advertised for a handyman to help with finishing the structure off. Charlie Shepherd applied for the job; he helped with the garage and then went into partnership with the Welches making shelving and cycle racks out of whatever job lots of material that could be acquired. The factory was a workshop behind a greengrocers in Ladypool Road, Sparkbrook.

The day was really saved however in September 1946 when an advert was seen in the Birmingham Mail offering for sale ex-government ammunition box liners 11" x 7" x 7" with drop on lids still in their original wrappings. They would make very neat, light, dustproof storage boxes, and they were available at 10d each. The Welches bought 1,000 and sold them at four for £1, 12 for 30 shillings or 100 for £12.

The dining room at home was cleared and the pair spent their evenings tying up parcels for the Post Office to collect the next morning. Postage then for a parcel weighing 15 lbs was 1/1d (5 1/2 p); if there was an order for more than 250 however, it paid to put them in a six foot railway container.

Above: Welconstruct Company Limited Catalogue, 1955.

Turnover in 1947 went up to £6,225 enabling the Welches to hire their first, part-time secretary. Until that time Pat Welch had done all his own typing under the reference PWW/LM (the LM stood for lui-meme - French for 'himself'). Pat had used an old Bar Lock typewriter that had separate keys for upper and lower case letters - something which he later claimed spoiled his typing technique so much he would always have trouble with a conventionally laid out keyboard.

In 1950, having already withdrawn from active participation in the business, E A Welch technically passed the company to his son. Welconstruct continued its growth operating out of a succession of offices in the centre of Birmingham: Upper Priory, Grenville Buildings - Cherry Street, Martineau Street, Carrs Lane and Camden House, Parade.

The firm was still selling its black ammunition box liners which were obtained from A C Hurlock Ltd which had rented a small island in the Thames which it piled high with boxes. The supply lasted until the mid 1950s. A C

Hurlock was incidentally originally the makers of the AC car and went on to make the well remembered invalid three wheeler.

Welconstruct was also buying bin units from W H Dixon in Broseley and with that decision the firm found itself focused on becoming a merchant rather than a manufacturer.

Clothes lockers were by now being obtained from various sources in addition to the firm's own brand. The first ones made by Welconstruct were built from 14 gauge flattened Anderson Shelter sheets: they weighed 100 lbs each and were according to Pat Welch 'dreadful'. A hundred were sent to Kodak's and they were all sent back. Some customers were however persuaded to keep them.

Pat Welch would recall going out as a lorry driver's mate with Arnold Purll and delivering a load of lockers to the Leicester Mercury newspaper offices. The locker doors were

Below: *Shelving supplied and installed in Bates Shop circa 1960.*

fitted with pin hinges which fell out as they were carried across the yard leaving a trail of hinges and doors.

Besides his stints as a lorry driver's mate Pat also carried the sacks of circulars to Corporation Street Post Office each Saturday morning and did any 'Rep to Calls' visiting potential customers - in those days he could get a return ticket to Sheffield for eight shillings (40p) by catching an early train and getting a 'workman's return' to Burton and then another workman's return from Burton to Sheffield.

In 1949 Pat and his part-time secretary left Upper Priory and moved to roomier offices - 10 feet by 10 feet - in Cherry Street, offices which now boasted not only an electric light but also a telephone.

On 2nd August 1952 Welconstruct became a Limited Company. The first 'modern' Welconstruct catalogue was produced in 1955.

In the following half century the growth of the business, with the addition of subsidiary companies, would be quite considerable, with total sales reaching £48m at its highest point.

Although it fell to him to lead the company, Pat Welch was never an entrepreneur - he lacked the adventurous trading spirit, the innovation and the engineering skills of his father. Welconstruct never set out to acquire other companies, but they were off-loaded by others who found the strains, and the failures, of business too much to carry. Welconstruct was meant to be a pot-shot at socialist commerce - it never hit the bull's eye, but scored in one or two of the outer rings.

It is that pot-shot which might give an interest to what is, otherwise, a normal trading company. Welconstruct lacked the courage, or retained the sense of ownership, which could have turned it into a thoroughly socialist

Above: Early Welconstruct Exhibition Stand.

enterprise, but it has stood within the aura of dissent which is the lasting memory of Old Birmingham. It was also the time when the ideas of the Company were able to bud and flower and, at times, even fruit.

No dividends were paid to shareholders, but 10% of the profits were paid into a charitable trust, with 10% also distributed to employees on the basis of one share for each year worked for the company, regardless of rank or responsibility.

Employees in Welconstruct were allowed an 'Expedition Day' each year when they could 'do something they have always wanted to do.'

Employees at the Telford factories enjoyed paid sick leave on equal terms with office staff.

A separate company, Parade Medical Ltd, was established to enable employees to take advantage of private medical care within three weeks. This was virtually non-contributory, but employees who did not accept the concept of private medicine were free not to join.

Grimmitt Finance Limited enabled employees to receive loans at rates well below normal bank charges. It also enabled customers to take extended credit whilst 'Nancy's Bank' enabled 'subs' to be enjoyed before the end of the month.

Christmas gifts were given to suppliers rather than customers; hampers were given to all employees and pensioners. (Pensions for all were introduced in the 1960s)

Company outings included flights to Paris, Amsterdam, Bruges, and a weekend in Majorca was arranged as a training course for all employees.

'Policies and Practices' was a document set out in full each year, regularly up-dated, and distributed at an

This page: Grenville Building, Cherry Street (top), and 35 Carrs Lane (offices over the Gunsmith's shop) former homes of the Welconstruct Group.

occasion when any questions could be asked and any complaints made.

The use of clichés in any writing, and illegible signatures on letters, were frowned upon, but the company took a liberal attitude towards split infinitives. Parties, of one sort or another, were arranged Winter and Summer. The Open Plan office was completely open to all - starting with the Managing Director and even including the Accountant.

It was never regarded as an idealist company, but with its growth and its profits, was actually a proof of its realism.

It was never a 'Family Company'; Tim Welch, after working as a live-in barman in EC4 became a rep; Kate Welch, having worked at Lucas's looks after Grimmitt Finance; Marjorie Welch became a Director - but it was her unstinted support which enabled the company to exist at the cost of her own interests and abilities. The company, in many ways, supported and served Birmingham and its various Institutions as well as others outside the city.

Waves of furniture

Whatever was going through the mind of a young man aboard HMS Diadem in 1943 as the ship battled its way north to Russia through ice, U-boat packs and German bombers it's unlikely that he was anticipating returning to Birmingham to become a self made millionaire. Yet that is exactly what Ted Cooke did.

Today Erdington based Cookes Furniture Ltd has one of the most prestigious furniture stores in Britain. The store in Goosemoor Lane features a huge range of products, an equally large annual turnover and more than a hundred employees. The long journey from Murmansk matelot to Midlands millionaire has been a remarkable one for Ted Cooke.

Ted Cooke started out in business for himself in November 1946. Edward Ronald Cooke was born on 29th November 1924, in Church Lane, Aston. His mother,

Mabel Cartwright was born in Boston, Lincolnshire, and then moved to Birmingham during the first world war where she met and married Edward Cooke from Aston.

Before the second world war young Ted Cooke trained as a tool setter working for Dunlop in Erdington. Ted had failed his 11 plus and left school at the age of 14 with no qualifications and, according to him, no ambition at all. Within three days of leaving school however he was at a factory lathe as an apprentice fitter and turner earning 12 shillings and sixpence a week.

When war broke out in 1939 Ted was paid to be a fire spotter in Erdington, watching for German bombers targeting the Dunlop factory. The wish to take a shot at the Luftwaffe by way of revenge might have led to Ted signing up for the RAF, but Ted always had a fascination for the sea.

Despite being in a reserved occupation, rather than wait to be called up he volunteered to join the Royal Navy, aged 18 in 1942. Modestly he says he joined up because of his love for the sea, he didn't want to risk being called into the army, and because he liked the uniform! At that age he didn't stop to think about the danger. And there would be plenty of danger ahead for the young sailor.

Top: Founder, Edward 'Ted' Cooke.
Above centre: Ted and Alicia Cooke on their Wedding day, 19th December 1945. *Below and right:* Jockey Road Post Office before being converted to Cooke & Son, 1970, and right, conversion completed in 1971.

After being sent to Roedean, the exclusive girls school which had been commandeered by the navy for training, Ted was posted as a petty officer electric artificer aboard HMS Diadem, an anti-aircraft cruiser, escorting convoys to Russia. The task was one of the most dangerous of the war.

The trips beyond Norway and Finland to reach Russia's northern ports had a five day turn around, dropping off arms and food. Twenty ships travelled together in convoy. HMS Diadem's job was to try and deflect attacks on the merchantmen by German U-boats and planes. At times it was so cold on deck that the sea water from the waves would turn to ice, and bare flesh would stick to metal railings.

Though the Diadem did come under fire, and was hit, fortunately Ted was unhurt and unlike others on the Murmansk run never had to abandon ship and take to the lifeboats, or worse swim for it.

Life expectancy for those who found themselves adrift in the sea at minus 30 degrees was just three minutes; and during an attack ships could not stop to pick up survivors from sunken vessels. Though Ted would pass through the ordeal of convoy duty unscathed many others gave their lives to provide the food and munitions which would help prevent the Soviet Union being crushed by Hitler's seemingly unstoppable armies. Nature in the form of violent freezing seas, the Luftwaffe and the German navy, the Kriegsmarine, made the experience of convoy duty truly the stuff of nightmares.

Ted witnessed planes crashing and exploding when attempting to land on aircraft carriers. And he saw boats hit and sunk. One night a hurricane hit the Diadem with such force that depth charges broke loose on deck, flattening railings

Top: The old Stone Laundry in 1934.
Above: Goosemoor Lane before construction.

and sending life jackets and all manner of other things over the side of the ship.

But things were about to change. D-day found Ted with the fleet moored off the coast of France supporting the Allied landings which would herald the end of the war.

Surprisingly, despite his frightening wartime experiences, Ted fell in love with the sea. In later years he would have his own boat moored at Christchurch, Dorset. The sea however was not his only love affair.

It was during his service with the Royal Navy that Ted met his wife, Alicia, on a call to the docks at Newcastle on Tyne. Alicia Finlay lived nearby and the pair met at a dance. They married on 19th December 1945 and made their home in temporary accommodation in Walmley Ash Road, Walmley, Sutton Coldfield.

After leaving the Royal Navy in 1946 Ted Cooke received £75 demob money, cash he intended to use to start up his own business rather than to go back to being a tool setter permanently.

After a year with Dunlop Ted set up a book lending round with two friends from work. They called the business the 'Fireside Library'. He bought a selection of books using his demob money and established himself in Mere Green and Falcon Lodge areas of Sutton Coldfield

buying new books for between 7s 6d and 1Os 6d each and renting them out for 6d a week, moving the travelling library around in a three-wheeler Reliant until graduating to an Austin Mini van in the 1960s. As a side line Ted also made strong leather shopping bags out of kits and sold these to his customers.

In retrospect it is obvious that Ted Cooke had been wasted as an engineer. He was one of life's natural entrepreneurs, a man born to be a businessman, someone who revelled in doing deals, meeting people and being his own boss. It was hard work, but Ted thrived on it.

Top: *Cooke & Son's Goosemoor Lane showroom, 1982.*
Above right: *Cooke & Son after expansion in 1991.*

Ted's two partners soon fell by the wayside unable to keep up with him. With his outgoing personality Ted was liked and respected by his customers. As their needs expanded so did the goods he could supply. If a customer asked if he could supply them with clothes and household items on credit - he would. More than fifty years later people are still coming into the store and recalling Ted visiting them on his credit round. Old customers, their children and even their grandchildren are still buying from Cookes today, a family business they can trust.

By the late 1950s Ted abandoned the library business to concentrate on haberdashery and other household goods. He used the Bell and Nicholson warehouse in Birmingham as his main supplier. In this way Ted built up a very strong and lucrative credit round. As the popularity of fitted carpets came into fashion, he quickly responded to the trend. He supplied samples, the actual carpets and then fitted them himself.

In the late 1960s because of the growing boom in fitted carpets Ted concentrated on this part of his business.

Until then the business had been run from Ted and Alicia's home in Walmley and later Boldmere. Alicia supported her husband on his credit rounds. She called at customers' houses, often taking their daughter Eleanor, born in 1947, along with her.

The post war years were perfect. Prime Minister Harold Macmillan was right when he declared that people had never had it so good. Folk who had made do with lino could now afford a carpet for the first time. And those who had made do with a carpet square now demanded fitted carpets.

So successful would the carpet business become that in 1971 Ted bought an old post office in Jockey Road Sutton Coldfield and knocked it down within hours to make way for new premises. So quick was the change that people were queuing up trying to cash postal orders whilst the bulldozers moved in.

Above: Graham Cooke, Cheif Executive, Alicia Cooke, Director, and Ted Cooke, Chairman celebrate the completion of the expansion programme to their Goosemoor Lane showroom, 1991. *Below:* Cookes 85,000 sq ft showroom, 2004.

Ted's son, Graham, was born in 1952. He joined his father, in 1972, after he had attended Carnegie college, Leeds. Both sold to customers, delivered furniture and fitted carpets. Alicia Cooke helped in the shop and joined her husband and son on buying trips. The credit round was now sold to enable the family to concentrate on carpets and furniture. Carpet sales, however, began to decrease as furniture increased in popularity. A small amount of furniture was sold from catalogues and brochures whilst Ted had the credit round, however, the Jockey Road Shop had plenty of room to display furniture for sale. Though 80 per cent of the business had been in carpet sales the new shop extensions enabled even more furniture to be sold.

The Cookes set about improving their furniture range offering an increasing choice of brand names backed by the kind of personal service that would become their hallmark. The business now became Cooke and Son Furniture Ltd.

Cookes has always been renowned for its high quality furniture. Though choice was limited at first it soon expanded as further accounts were opened. Now there was a remarkable choice available.

By 1974, even though the bulk of their sales was still in the carpet side of the business the Cookes made the decision to concentrate solely in furniture retailing in the future. From then on the business began to snowball.

The Jockey Road shop was one of the first retailers to offer customers a discount. They were offered 20% off their furniture and customers loved it.

Cooke & Son bought the old Stone's laundry premises , a three acre site in Goosemoor Lane Erdington from the Birmingham co-op in 1982. The rundown 12,000 sq ft building was turned into a showroom in just three months opening its doors for business on 22nd June 1982. Seven years later a series of extensions had seen the premises grow to 65,000 sq ft and more extensions would follow.

This page: *Cookes Furniture Warehouse (top) and an interior view of the showroom, 2004.*

Another store was opened in Christchurch in 1993 and to coincide with this the business changed its name from Cooke and Son to Cookes Furniture Ltd.
In 1996, to celebrate 50 years of business, Cookes entered the 'Retailer of the Year' competition for the first and only time. Few were surprised when in 1997 Cookes carried off the award.

Cookes has two showrooms, one in Erdington and one in Christchurch. There are also two Renka showrooms, one in Sutton Coldfield and one in Christchurch. Cookes also own Romo Reproduction Furniture, a manufacturing business which produces the finest quality yew and mahogany furniture. Not only do they supply Cookes stores, they also supply a selection of other prestigious independent retail outlets across the country.

One measure of customer demand is the size of today's Erdington showroom. When it was bought in 1982 it covered a 'mere' 12,000 sq ft, since then the building has grown to a huge 85,000 sq ft.

Today all the stores sell a broad mix of mid to upmarket brand name furniture to customers, the majority living within a 50 mile radius of each store. Cookes also do contract work abroad supplying yacht clubs and hotels with furniture.

One of only twelve independent family businesses of its kind in the country in the future Cookes looks to open even more stores between Birmingham and Christchurch.

Despite the passing decades Ted Cooke is still full of energy. He married again to Pauline Cooke in 1998, the ceremony taking place on the island of Mauritius and followed, appropriately enough for an ex-navy man, by a round the world cruise. He still goes into the flagship store, in Goosemoor Lane, everyday, unless he is on one of his frequent trips to his house in Spain. However he

is no longer actively involved in business decisions or in selling; his job is to add all the figures at the end of the day and compare them to previous ones!

Ted's son Graham Cooke is now Chief Executive of the group. He divides his time between Birmingham and Christchurch.

Eleanor Barton, Graham Cookes sister, is in charge of all the PR activity for the company. Cookes is one of the main sponsors for the local Sutton Fun Run which Eleanor organises as the company's way of giving something back to the community. Down in Christchurch Cookes also sponsors the local Regatta festival.

Cookes Furniture Ltd is now a third generation business. The longer term outlook of this family business is in the hands of Graham and his three daughters who all work in the business. Michelle graduated from university in 2001 and is now merchandising manager. She constantly attends furniture shows and factory visits all over Europe to ensure Cookes stock the latest quality designs. Vanessa graduated in 2003 and is now working in marketing, closely assessing the best way to market the furniture bought by Michelle. Jennifer, still studying for her degree, works in the company as much as possible, ready to begin full time work, alongside her father and sisters, on her graduation in 2006.

Through hard work and ingenuity the outlook for Cookes Furniture and the Cooke family is today brighter by far than could ever have been imagined by that young sailor making his perilous way through Arctic seas so many years ago.

Top: Ted Cooke (centre) with daughter Eleanor and son Graham. *Below:* Chief Executive Graham Cooke and daughters Jennifer (left), Vanessa (back right) and Michelle.

A fitting success

The Savekers Group with its hundred-plus strong workforce based in Aldridge Road, Perry Barr today manufactures architectural metalwork for architects, designers, cabinet makers, builders merchants, glass merchants and shop fitters. Its products can be seen all across Britain in offices, hotels bars and restaurants, shops, banks, building societies and post offices.

How the Group's Managing Director Dani Saveker came to find herself at the head of a prominent Midlands manufacturing firm, and the history of that unique company, is a long and fascinating tale.

The firm was founded in 1903 by Thomas Saveker. Basing himself in Parliament Street, Aston, Thomas undertook small joinery contracts and shop fitting.

In the 1920s the business moved to an old needle factory on Aston Brook Street where it now established metalworking, brass polishing and antique bronze.

The firm incorporated in the 1930s. During the early part of that decade one of the first electroplating companies was purchased and the company began chrome plating. Gas and electric light fittings were now produced under the trade name Ceilite.

By now the company was employing some 120 staff, two of Thomas Saveker's sons Herbert, ('Bert'), and Frank now joined him.

The factory was extended, building the premises across Aston Brook facing Phillips Street. By the close of the 1930s Thomas' third son, Ronald Charles Saveker had also joined the company.

Ron however, was soon called away for war service and would not return until 1945.

During the second world war T Saveker Ltd produced 75 different parts for Spitfire fighter planes, over 280 parts for Lancaster bombers, parts for Sten guns and over a quarter of a million stirrup pumps.

The factory survived the war almost unscathed. Two incendiary bombs however fell on the plating shop, one went straight into a vat and the other bounced off a roof beam and then into the vat - both bombs were extinguished by the vat's contents. Another incident was a high explosive bomb which fell into the ground close to a sunken air raid shelter in the factory yard but which did not explode. The very next

Top left: Founder Thomas Saveker.
Above: An early Saveker vehicle.

night another bomb was heard to fall nearby and both bombs exploded; fortunately the area had been evacuated and no-one was hurt - bowed metal window frames facing the crater however remained a reminder of that night until the building was demolished in 1998.

Towards the end of the war, in April 1944, Bert's son Thomas Derek Saveker would join the company. Derek was still two weeks short of his 15th birthday when he quit grammar school and started work as a sorter of drills and screws and as an issuer of smaller tools under the store keeper George Weetman.

In 1951 Thomas Saveker 'The Governor' was the guest speaker at a celebratory dinner for A Edmonds who were celebrating 50 years in business: the following day, aged 73, the company founder died leaving his son Bert as Chairman.

Unfortunately Bert Saveker himself would die suddenly in June 1960 aged just 56, leaving his son Derek to run the company. During Bert's nine year tenure the company had undergone a gradual evolution, further developing its in-house design function for markets such as light fittings, food and merchandising displays.

Ron's son, Michael James Saveker joined the company in 1961. Frank became Chairman in 1960, with his brother Ron and himself remaining as directors until they both retired at the age of 70 years old in 1975 and 1981 respectively.

New names now began to appear. Philip Walters joined the company in 1973 working for Fritz Sommer, the firm's fourth Director, as his

Top: A Saveker family photograph.
Above: *Early Saveker Suspension Light Fittings.*

assistant and progress clerk. That year also saw the first of the Villers family join the company with Mick Villers starting on 15th October. Philip Walters would subsequently become one of the firm's Executive Directors. In the mid to the late 1970s the company's emphasis began to move towards smaller 'kit' type products, and components such as barrier rails and bar fittings.

in total lived in a tiny terraced house in Holte Road, Aston, in a religious order which dedicates itself to a life of prayer whilst working alongside ordinary people in manual jobs.

Thomas Martin Saveker, Derek's son, joined the company full time in 1981 following his university studies having gained a degree in production engineering.

Perhaps one of the most unusual members of staff at Savekers in those years were two of its works cleaners. In the late 1970s the firm got what can best be described as a heavenly surprise when they advertised for a part time cleaner. The only applicant for the job was a nun.

Sister Cecelia, a member of the order of The Little Sisters of Jesus, was snapped up for the job. Nor was Sister Cecelia the only member of her order to work for Savekers. Another nun, Sister Anna, stepped in to do the cleaning whilst Sister Cecelia travelled to France for medical treatment. Sister Anna, a 41 year old former nurse, proved just as popular with the men on the factory floor as had Sister Cecelia. Four nuns

Top: *Electric light pendants and standard lamps.*
Above: *Ron (left) and Frank Saveker sons of the founder Thomas Saveker.*

Martin, today's company Chairman, had been a regular visitor to the factory since his early childhood. He came into the office on most Saturdays with his father, sometimes going to the packing department and getting the staff there to set up timber runs on which to race his model cars. When he was a little older some of the men would tell him about years gone by: his favourite was Bill Hobbs in the brass shop. Bill used to tell Martin about the arguments between his father and Martin's grandfather: old Mr Hobbs either resigned or was fired most Friday afternoons but always reappeared for work on Monday - man management was rather different in those days.

Catherine Owen, today's Production Administrator joined the company from school in 1983 as a progress chaser on £30 a week on a three month trial. The trial has lasted more than two decades! During the 1980s she would witness the company's design function to become ever more responsive to customers' demand for bespoke products. By the 1990s the company was striving to further develop its unique bespoke service by enhancing and improving its designs and production facilities through the use of new technology.

When Derek Saveker retired his son Martin took over as Chairman. Martin's cousin Dani Saveker started work for the company in 1995 after obtaining a degree in Design & Marketing.

Dani's earliest memories of the company at the Philip Street site also went back to her childhood. She would be brought to the factory by her mother and often pop in to visit her grandfather and Uncle Mike. At that time she was around five years old and would enter the building through its large green doors and walk up its big stone staircase. Dani was in awe of the building, yet the distinctive smell was always friendly and familiar.

Derek Saveker would make the most amazing paper aeroplanes for his second cousin and throw them across his office; he also taught her that most important of executive skills - how to flick rubber bands across a room and into a waste paper bin! If Dani was really lucky however, she got to spend half an hour or so in the packing area, counting screws and putting them into bags once a box had been found for her to stand on.

The first proper work Dani undertook for the company was when her cousin, Tony Saveker, was taken ill with pneumonia and she covered for him in the purchasing department. After joining the firm full time she worked on product development before subsequently working in every department.

In 1997 the company relocated to its current premises in Aldridge Road, Perry Bar, closing the Phillips Street site. During the course of the move Philip Walters suffered a heart attack and as a consequence could not continue as Works Director.

After so long in one place the move was emotional for all involved. Philip, Martin, Dani and her mother Diane closed the old building for the final time after walking through its empty spaces reminiscing about old times.

Following Dani Saveker's reorganisation of the production department in 2001 she was offered a directorship. In September 2001 Martin Saveker and his parents announced their plans to sell their shares in the company. Dani immediately knew that she wanted to take over and acquire their shareholding. Within a month of their announcement she had managed to create a plan of action for the shares

February 2002 saw Martin Saveker resign as Managing Director. The Board and shareholders appointed Dani to replace him

Mike Saveker retired two months later whilst Tony Saveker left to take a new direction in his career. The current management team was appointed in May 2002.

The future should have been bright, and it was - but not quite in the way Dani had expected. On 7th October 2002 Dani was woken by a telephone call announcing that the factory was on fire. Some 15 fire engines were in attendance. The plating plant was no more and major damage had been sustained to the factory roof.

Top: Bert Saveker (left) and son Derek.
Above: One of Savekers window displays; a chocolate box stand.

The origin of the fire was never conclusively identified. When switched on automatically in the early hours of Monday 7th October the resultant overheating of the plating plant caused the fire.

Over the following months a new roof, newly clad walls, a new sign and a new heating system were installed whilst extensive cleaning took place. In May 2003 the previous Works Director Philip Walters opened the new £250,000 plating plant in time to celebrate the centenary of this remarkable company, a centenary also marked by its launch of a new corporate identity.

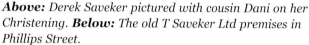

Above: *Derek Saveker pictured with cousin Dani on her Christening.* **Below:** *The old T Saveker Ltd premises in Phillips Street.*

The new logo and name style however maintained strong links with the company's history by using elements from Ceilite, one of its original trade name designs.

In addition to giving itself a makeover the company also decided to mark its centenary by giving something back to the community. Throughout its centenary year a percentage of each 100th order received each week was donated to the Midlands-based Acorns Children's Hospital Trust - a charity which cares for children who are unlikely to live to adulthood and offers support for their families as well as providing respite and emergency care at each of its hospices in addition to round the clock support at home through its community teams.

With its Group structure now complete, and led by Dani Saveker, the company still stocks standard products but is moving ever closer towards conceptual design and the provision of total solutions to clients needs. With an impressive customer base made up from well known high street names such as Marks & Spencer, Dorothy Perkins, Selfridges and Harrods Savekers works with its customers from the initial conception through to the completion of each project.

The Group is now able to provide high quality bespoke joinery and a range of other products and services. Their aim is to develop the Group through further acquisitions and build on the foundations laid down by Thomas, Bert and Derek Saveker.

The company still has support and involvement from family members and past directors.

The company has now broken into the export trade supplying balustrades to hotels and palatial homes in the Far East and hopes to penetrate the European market in the near future.

Hot on the heels of the Groups formation Savekers acquired the joinery and metalwork business of West Bromwich shopfitting and display equipment manufacturers Pride in Design in a move which has instantly expanded the company's product and service portfolios as well as its manufacturing capabilities.

Meanwhile, in a welcome return to the past, the company has decommissioned its automated telephone answering system and put real people answering the phone. It may cost a little more but there can be no substitute for providing customers with a traditional, and above all genuinely personal, service.

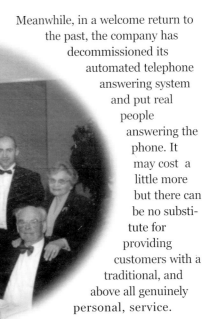

The joinery side of Pride in Designs business was significant and has been set up as 'Sav Joinery', based at Walsall Road, Perry Barr.

Top left: The company's new electroplating plant opened in 2003 by ex Works Director Philip Walters.
Top right: Philip Walters and Dani Saveker at the opening ceremony of the new plant. **Above:** Centenary celebration for the family and support team.

Hot off the presses

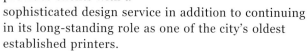

The name Silk & Terry Ltd is one which has been well known in Birmingham since the reign of Queen Victoria. Since 1962 the company has been based in Warstock Road. Today the company is a supplier of computer typesetting and print and also provides clients with a sophisticated design service in addition to continuing in its long-standing role as one of the city's oldest established printers.

In 1895 determination to succeed and enthusiasm for the craft of printing led Sidney H. Terry & Ernest William Silk to leave their jobs with Cond Bros. of Paternoster Row, Birmingham and found their own firm of Silk & Terry in two small rooms in premises at 130 Edmund Street.

At the time Mr Terry was 32 and Mr Silk 24, the former having been apprenticed as a compositor and the latter employed as a clerk. Mr. Silk had also had some experience travelling, selling printers blanks and other goods for Conds' 'Fancy Department'. This experience stood him in good stead later when he concentrated on the selling side of the business of Silk & Terry so leaving his partner to supervise production.

The two partners each subscribed £250 as capital and agreed to limit their salary to 50/- per week until such times as the business was firmly established.

Their original equipment consisted of a Crown folio 'Golding Jobber' - at that time was the best in platen

*Top: Silk & Terry circa 1904. **Below:** An early 20th century photograph found in Silk & Terry's records.*

machines - and a few display faces of type including Old Style, Caxton Black and some founts of Sans Serif.

Printing at this time was recovering from what was probably the worst period in all the 500 years since its introduction into England. In the very old days there were four faces of style, and however they were arranged they did not look too bad. But at this later period most printing works were equipped with many small founts of unrelated and often terrible design.

All type was set by hand. Line and half-tone work was only in the experimental stage and illustrations were mostly reproduced from wood engravings or Lithographed

All platen machines have treadles attached and even the cylinders were supplied with a wooden handle which could be fitted to the flywheel.

A third member of the original staff was Mr Terry's 18 year old brother Edmund James 'Jim' who had also been employed by Cond Bros.

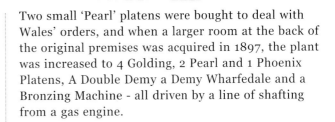

At first, most of the typesetting was done by Sidney Terry and the machining by Jim. but it was not long before Jim was showing such an aptitude for designing and 'typography' that the first machine minder, a man named Bradbury was engaged, allowing Jim to concentrate on the creative side of the business.

One of the earliest of the firm's customers was Wales & Son, bedstead manufacturers and without the encouragement and help given by Mr. F C. Adie of that firm it would have been impossible for the two partners to have developed the business so quickly.

Two small 'Pearl' platens were bought to deal with Wales' orders, and when a larger room at the back of the original premises was acquired in 1897, the plant was increased to 4 Golding, 2 Pearl and 1 Phoenix Platens, A Double Demy a Demy Wharfedale and a Bronzing Machine - all driven by a line of shafting from a gas engine.

By 1898 it can be said that Silk & Terry were a firm to be reckoned with in the Birmingham printing industry. Mr. W. H. Wilde and Mr. H. W. Bentley joined the firm in 1898 and 1899 respectively, although Mr. Bentley had previously been employed as a compositor & reader in 1896/7. In addition to the two partners there was now an office staff consisting of W. Watkin Gabb, H. B. Steele and H. W. Bentley, six Compositors, ten letterpress machine minders and a warehouse staff of seven. In 1899 further accommodation was rented from Messrs. AlIday Ltd. who had built a five storey building in Bread Street (now Cornwall Street) backing on to the Edmund Street premises and where

Top: Silk & Terry cica 1930s.
Left: Early advertising of catalogues.

considerably increased capacity. The main plant was driven from shafting coupled to a Tangye Gas Engine installed in the back basement and a subsidiary shaft supplied power to a line of platens. The Composing Department was on the right side of the balcony and the Binding Department on the left.

The reputation of the firm grew from year to year and a great quantity of important technical and catalogue work was produced for many large undertakings in the Midlands and London, particularly in the jewellery, bedstead, and engineering trades.

The firm had been early in the field with the halftone process and in 1898 had assisted with some of the earliest 3 and 4 colour process work in Birmingham, doing much of the early proofing for the Arthur Cox Illustrating Co.

In 1914 the Company could look forward to the future with confidence, but on November 4th, only 3 months

additional letterpress machinery and a lithographic plant were installed. The lithographic business of Messrs. Renaud was purchased and a quantity of very high quality colour lithography was produced chiefly for the brass foundry and bedstead trade.

By 1900 the business was rapidly growing and Mr. William Brooking was engaged as Works Manager with Mr. Wilde as his assistant. Two years later it was evident that larger and more convenient premises were necessary. It was, therefore, decided to build new works in Great Charles Street on land leased from the Colmore Estate. The new building was ready for occupation by Easter 1904.

The new premises consisted of a front block of four storeys with a large hall at the rear with one balcony running round and basements at the front and back of the building. An up to date letterpress and lithographic plant were installed with a

Top: A letter from EW Silk informing clients that despite an enemy air attack during the second world war Silk & Terry would be able to handle any work they may be entrusted with, also pictured is a thank you card sent out by the company to those who offered their sympathy to Silk & Terry during this period.
Right: Delicate fingers speedily turn words into metal printing type.

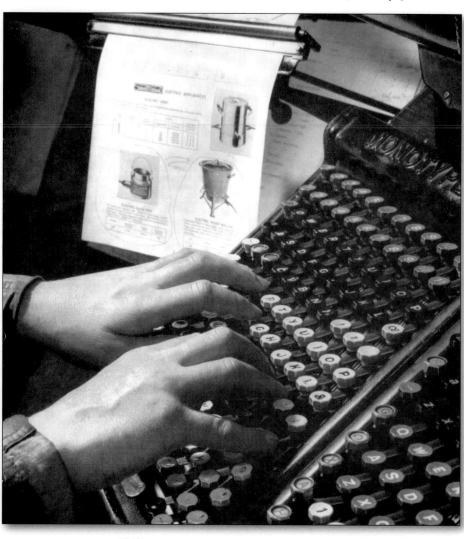

after the outbreak of the first World War, a disastrous fire occurred, which destroyed almost the whole of the interior of the building and its contents. The cause of the fire was never discovered, but the principals were determined to rebuild at the earliest possible moment.

All that could be salvaged was removed to temporary premises at the corner of Ludgate Hill and Great Charles St. and a few new machines and equipment were installed. Willing help was given by competitors in Birmingham and Coventry to replace work which had been destroyed and with the co-operation of customers, the immediate difficulties were overcome. The debris from the burnt-out building was quickly cleared enabling a number of machines to be sent to the makers for overhaul and rebuilding.

The premises were rebuilt with increased floor space by the addition of a second gallery and an extra storey at the front. The interior of the new building was almost entirely built of reinforced concrete. The original wooden floors being replaced throughout with concrete and an automatic sprinkler system installed, the benefit of which would become evident when the building was hit by fire bombs from German aircraft in 1940. The gas engine and shafting were discarded in favour of directly coupled electric motors.The new premises were ready for occupation in November 1915 only twelve months after the fire occurred. The war however had caused many of the men to be called to the colours and a portion of the factory was let to Vickers for the production of munitions.

In 1916 in order to raise new capital the business became a Limited Liability Company as Silk & Terry Ltd. The capital

Above: A 1958/9 Silk & Terry calendar.
Below: Craftsmanship on the printing machine.

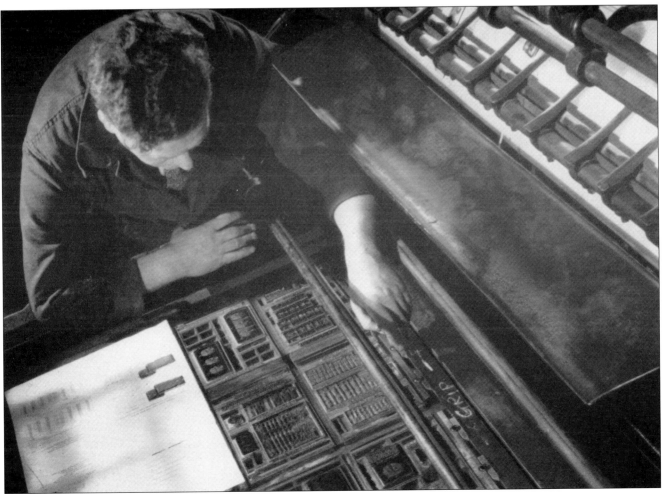

was £17,000 divided into 7,000 7% Cumulative Preference Shares and 10,000 Ordinary Shares of £1 each.

The building remained the joint property of Mr. Silk & Mr. Terry and was leased back to the Company at an annual rental of £750. The first Directors were E. W. Silk, Chairman & Joint Managing Director; S. H. Terry, Joint Managing Director, Mr W. H. Wilde and Mr. R. W. Lugsdin. The last named would die of illness in 1918 while on active service in France.

The longest serving member of the original team would be Jim Terry who would eventually clock up an astonishing sixty years with the firm. A tradition of long service would not be unusual: Mr HL Butler, the firm's technical representative, would spend more than half a century with the company as would Miss Clara Edgington, and bookbinder Mr F Gumery. Many other staff would stay with the firm for forty years or more.

In 1914, Jim had been appointed first instructor to the classes for printers' apprentices for two mornings and one evening per week.

Some of the members of the Master Printers Association had for many years realised that their apprentices were not

Above: A final check before printing. Top right: The finished sheets come off - Silk & Terry quality. Right: Silk & Terry's centenary lunch, 1995.

getting sufficient training, and they had approached the School of Art Committee to see if classes could be formed for their benefit. A large room in Margaret Street was placed at Jim Terry's disposal and he was instructed to order frames, press, type and general material sufficient for about a dozen apprentices. Twelve months afterwards a small 'Victoria' platen was added. The mornings were for practical work and the evenings for drawing and lettering.

When the first world war was over the classes were thrown open to young journeymen and became very crowded. A number of part-time teachers were engaged and Jim Terry's one evening was increased to four.

At one time there had been some opposition to the School as several classes for printers were held at the Technical School and it was rightly felt that all printing classes should be held in one building. It was eventually agreed however that the Art School was the most suitable place and Jim Terry was joined by two excellent craftsman: Mr Gill, of the Birmingham Printers on the monotype, and Mr. Cotterill of the Birmingham Gazette on the Linotype.

The School was fortunate in having Art Directors who were keenly interested in printing. Mr. Catherson-Smith under whom Jim Terry first served had helped William Morris with the drawings for the initials and illustrations for this famous books. Mr B J Fletcher who succeeded Mr Catherson-Smith had already built up one of the most noted printing schools at Leicester. He invited many special lecturers to come to Birmingham, and did much to increase the Popularity of the printing School.

In 1925 Jim Terry was invited to give all his time to the School but declined as he

Staff development would be crucial: leading to such accolades as the nomination of Ruth Hollins as a finalist for a nationally recognised print award. The emphasis on printing however, which had been the mainstay of the company for more than a hundred years, began to become a less significant part of the whole. Machinery had become outdated and a large capital investment needed. From having 23 employees in 1995 gradual redundancy reduced that number over the following six years whilst all the old printing machines were sold. The company now became a selling agency for loyal customers and kept a turnover of approaching £200,000.

felt under an obligation to Silk & Terry Ltd. which had allowed him sufficient time off for eleven years to conduct these classes, and he resigned so that a full time Instructor could be appointed.

The last of the Terry family to be involved in the business would be Chris Terry who retired as joint managing director in 1987. The Silk family line however would continue, with Michael Silk, now representing the third generation of his family, in the profession which had seen his grandfather EW Silk twice serve as president of the Master Printers Alliance, and his father WK Silk elected president of the Birmingham Master Printers Alliance.

It would fall to Michael Silk to have the honour of hosting Silk & Terry's celebratory luncheon, held in 1995, to mark the firm's centenary.

At various times the fourth generation of the Silk family worked for Silk & Terry - Suzanne and Rachel as designers and typesetters, though they are now self employed. In the late 1990s Alexander Silk worked for the firm for two years before moving on after having brought the company up to date by introducing it to computers.

The approach of the new millennium saw Silk & Terry Ltd begin to evolve in response to changing patterns of business.

Simultaneously, over the period from 1994 to 2003, a retail stationery business was developed which achieved an annual turnover of £300,000 before being sold off.

Above: The folding machine in Silk & Terry's finishing department. **Top right:** *Managing Director Mike Silk accepting an award.* **Below left:** *Ruth Hollins, a finalist of the print awards.* **Below:** *Silk & Terry Ltd's Warstock Road premises.*

The cuisine king from Hong Kong

In the centre of Birmingham at Holloway Circus, the roundabout serving as the gateway to Birmingham's Chinese quarter, is a Chinese pagoda. It took five years of discussions with the local planning department to get approval, but eventually the pagoda, hand-carved from solid granite and standing 40 ft high, was shipped in sections from China, where it had been created, to the United Kingdom and assembled on site. The pagoda was a gift from local entrepreneur Mr Wing Yip and his brothers, and a public thank you to the people of the city of Birmingham, the city which has made it possible for their business to become a remarkable success, and which has provided a home for them and their families.

Mr Woon Wing Yip arrived from Hong Kong by boat in 1959 with just ten pounds in his pocket and has since become one of the United Kingdom's most successful Chinese - businessmen. Indeed Mr Yip has become one of the most successful businessmen in any category.

These days it's easy to forget that not so very long ago Chinese restaurants and Chinese dishes were all but unknown in Britain. True there were a few Chinese restaurants, but these catered mostly for the small Chinese communities in our major cities rather than for the indigenous British. There were of course some Britons who were familiar with the delights of the Orient: many thousands of British servicemen, administrators and businessmen, had lived and worked in outposts of the Empire such as Hong Kong and other parts of the Far East, and those who had returned home long remembered the taste of Chinese cooking.

For most British folk however, Chinese food was either completely unknown or indeed something to make jokes about. In Britain simple meat and two veg was standard fare in most households. And as for a take-away, well that meant either fish and chips or maybe pie and peas - little else. Anyone who had predicted in the late 1950s that within a few decades every High Street in the land would boast at least one Chinese restaurant, never mind countless other previously unfamiliar foreign foods, well they would simply have been laughed at.

What did the British think of Chinese food forty years ago or more? It all sounded very strange. Didn't the Chinese eat one hundred year old eggs? And didn't they eat rice with everything instead of chips and mashed potato? If the British ate rice it was as a sweet pudding for afters: how unnatural we thought it to eat pudding with your main course.

And then there were those chop sticks. Why didn't the Chinese eat with a knife and fork like everyone else? How very odd. And how did they manage to get the food to their mouths using those awkward sticks of wood and not end up with grains of rice scattered all over the table?

Britain was soon going to discover the answers to all those questions, and in the process begin a love affair with Chinese food which has continued undiminished to this day. That love affair has transformed our High Streets and our diets - and in the process eroded Britain's gastronomic insularity, making the United Kingdom one of the most enjoyable places in the world to eat with its vast range of restaurants catering to every conceivable taste.

Above: Mr Woon Wing Yip, founder of Wing Yip pictured after receiving a Honarary Fellowship from Birmingham College of Food, Tourism and Creative Studies, 1995.

It is difficult now to recall the excitement and the culture shock when the British first went for a meal in a Chinese restaurant. For many it was the most adventurous thing they had ever done in their lives. The waiters were not English, would they be able to understand what we asked for? Then there was the anxiety of wondering whether one would be required to eat with chop sticks, and in the process made to look foolish; that anxiety soon turned to fascination with the mysteries of the menu once knives and forks were found to be laid out on the table. Would we dare to try some of those previously unheard of Chinese dishes, or take the easy way out and select steak and chips from the English end of the menu? Those who dared to try the unfamiliar soon discovered that they'd won more than simply the admiration of their dining companions.

Mr Woon Wing Yip is descended from the ancient Hakka family. The Hakka people are descended from the middle of China where civilisation began and the Hakka have spread across the globe as a result of war in their original homeland.

Arriving in London Mr Wing Yip intended to visit a friend who was arranging a job for him. However, after travelling for one month Mr Wing Yip arrived to find that his friend had moved away. He then went to Liverpool where the Liverpool Hakka Association found him a job - where he was quickly promoted to waiter because he could speak English. From there he moved to Hull for a short while.

Approximately two years later Wing and two business partners opened their own restaurant in a former tea shop in Clacton-on-Sea in Essex which they had bought for £500. Fortune smiled on the three partners as there was a Butlins camp opened just outside Clacton in 1962. The restaurants inside and outside the holiday camp served their last meal by 9.30 pm. People on holiday often wanted not only to eat later but also have a change and eat something different from the usual fare: Mr Wing Yip and his partners would stay open until midnight providing hungry folk with what back then were very novel Chinese dishes. With up to 8,000 holiday makers and up to 2,000 staff at the height of the season at the holiday camp the two restaurant owners from Hong Kong found they had a thriving business on their hands, one which was soon generating enough money to expand.

That first Chinese restaurant in Clacton was quickly followed by the opening of two others and one take-away in East Anglia. The second restaurant was in Ipswich where there was a nearby American airbase. The Americans were already familiar with Chinese food, and the

Left: The first Wing Yip shop in Digbeth, 1970.

restaurant became popular with them as a place to take their girl friends for an evening out.

By the late 1960s however, Mr Wing Yip had tired of serving sweet and sour and chow mein for late night customers and was looking for new business opportunities. Rather than being a restaurateur himself he thought instead he might do better by supplying the many new Chinese restaurants which were by now springing up all over Britain. It was to prove to be an inspired decision.

Mr Wing Yip had been followed to the UK by his brother Sammy, who until then had worked at the Hilton Hotel in Hong Kong. In 1970 Mr Wing Yip and his brother opened their first specialist Chinese grocers, located in the heart of Birmingham. At the store at 135 Digbeth over a thousand different products were sold, initially to local Chinese families for cooking their traditional dishes at home, as well as to restaurants and take-aways. The first Wing Yip store employed fewer than ten staff.

But it was not all plain sailing. In those early days the business experienced problems with the UK Customs and the port health authorities. Officials did not always know

what the Oriental foodstuffs were, and did not understand why it was important to be bringing them into the country. Happily however such cultural differences are now a thing of the past.

Mr Wing Yip soon became the UK's leading Chinese grocer. In 1975 the store moved to larger premises in Coventry Street.

Top: *A view inside the first Wing Yip store.*
Above: *Shoppers inside a Wing Yip supermarket.*

In 1977 the two brothers, Mr Wing Yip and Sammy, were joined by a third brother Lee Sing Yap who had owned a store in Jamaica, before coming to the United Kingdom to join the expanding business.

The Wing Yip Centre in Nechells was completed in 1992. Today, in the 21st century, the business operates from four key sites - Birmingham, Manchester, Cricklewood and Croydon; the company employs more than 300 staff.

Each Wing Yip superstore is built in a convenient location just outside each city centre. The Birmingham store incorporates a wide range of amenities including a Chinese restaurant, a Chinese dentist, doctor, travel agent, accountant, solicitor, bank and printer.

The company currently supplies most of the UK's 2,000 plus Chinese restaurants as well as catering for the domestic shopper. By dividing the stores into two sections Wing Yip has successfully managed to meet the requirements of both types of client.

For the consumer Wing Yip provides a one stop shop, providing secure parking with lighting for motorists travelling from afar: research has shown that customers will travel up to 50 miles to shop at a Wing Yip store.

Nor are Wing Yip products sold only in its own stores. The retail own-brand sauce range launched in 1999 can be found in leading supermarkets including Waitrose. Flavours include black bean, spicy Szechuan, sweet and sour and Chinese curry.

Wing Yip imports products directly from the Far East, with each store now stocking over 2,500 items ranging from cooking utensils, including woks and chinaware, to a vast selection of oriental sauces, meats, fish, vegetables, rice, herbs and spices as well as more unusual and unfamiliar products such as chickens' feet.

Each Wing Yip outlet prides itself on personal service and customer help desks are clearly visible on entering each of the four stores.

Help to pack bags and load trolleys or cars is a standard service. At the Birmingham store a telephone ordering service enables account customers, including busy restaurants and hotels, to receive orders delivered direct to their doors.

Mr Wing Yip is Chairman of the company; Sammy Yap is responsible for the trading side of the business whilst Lee Sing Yap is the Director responsible for running the Manchester superstore.

Of the next generation of sons and nephews Henry Yap based at the Birmingham headquarters is a qualified solicitor as well as Director of the legal, administration and property side of the business practiced in the UK and Hong Kong for over 10 years before returning to work in the company. Albert Yip is a qualified pharmacist as well as possessing a degree in business management: his role is as Assistant Store Manager with responsibility for purchasing, based at the Wing Yip Centre in Croydon. Brian Yip has a degree in banking and finance and is a fully qualified chartered accountant: he is responsible for W Wing Yip International Trading Ltd and is based in Birmingham. Ennevor Yap has a business management degree and is assistant Store Manager in Manchester.

Left: A prominent and familiar feature to the people of Birmingham, this Pagoda situated just outside Birmingham China Town was hand carved from in China from solid granite. Standing at 40 feet tall this beautiful piece of art was generously presented as a gift to the people of Birmingham from Mr Wing Yip and his brothers as a gesture of thanks to the City that has enabled their business to become a success and providing a home for their family.

Mr Wing Yip and his brothers have also set up the W Wing Yip and Brothers Charitable Trust which is fully financed by the family and business. Over many years the Trust has helped Chinese Sunday schools and made donations towards the many Chinese Associations throughout the UK on a regular basis during the years. The Trust also donates money to the Prince's Trust

The family has also set up the W Wing Yip & Brothers Bursaries whereby they sponsor 30-35 Chinese university students per annum as well as sponsoring two Chinese students to study at Cambridge and one English student from Cambridge to study in China. All staff members, whatever nationality, whose children are studying at university receive financial assistance on an annual basis from the Trust.

Ten years later Bob Brittain, a experienced qualified chartered accountant joined the company from Deloitte, Haskins, Sells and has recently retired after over 20 years service. He now continues to work part time as company secretary. The recruitment of Rod Honess as Managing Director who has held senior management positions in public companies and Chris Torbe as Financial Director who is a qualified chartered accountant has further strengthened the company.

The operating business is separate from the family's investments. W Wing Yip & Brothers Trading Group which controls the stores is managed quite separately from the W Wing Yip Brothers and Property and Investments which oversees the family's property portfolio. The founder, Mr Wing Yip, however remains as Chairman and his brothers are also directors of both companies.

*Top: Mr Wing Yip (centre) and his brothers Mr Sammy Yap (left) and Mr Lee Sing Yap. **Above right:** Wing Yip stocks the largest variety of authentic Chinese and Oriental sauces in the UK. **Right:** A familiar landmark to thousands of people, the Wing Yip Oriental Arch forms the entrance to both Wing Yip Birmingham and Wing Yip Croydon.*

Mr Wing Yip and his family place great emphasis on the benefits of children receiving a good education.

Yet for all his triumphs Mr Woon Wing Yip remains a quiet modest man in the best Confucian tradition. Unlike others who have made fortunes introducing new grocery and products to Britain he has never sought personal publicity; he is not mentioned in Who's Who; he does not play an active role in the Midlands business community, nor make large donations to political parties, though he is a generous if anonymous benefactor to the community.

'There is an old Chinese saying - 'never ask a hero where he comes from' says Mr Yip. In England there is another saying: 'Don't judge a man by his words, but by his deeds'.

By anyone's standards Mr Wing Yip's deeds have ensured him a place amongst the most prominent and respected of Birmingham's sons; they have made him a man whose influence extends far beyond the city across the whole of the United Kingdom, not only to every town but to virtually every home.

For the future the company intends to open even more Wing Yip superstores to cover the whole of the United Kingdom. As for what happened to that £10 which Wing Yip had in his pocket in 1959, today his business has an annual turnover of an incredible £70 million plus substantial income from the property side of the business. Mr Wing Yip is the only Chinese in the UK to be mentioned in the top 50 rich list in the West Midlands and top 1,000 national rich list.

Left: A current family photograph.
Bottom: Wing Yip, Nechells, Birmingham.

From bedknobs to bombers

Astonishingly the most abundant metal on Earth is aluminium. But, although it may be the most common, this metal was all but unknown two hundred years ago since it occurs naturally only as an oxide. So rare was the metal that the aluminium tableware used by the top table at the court of Napoleon II of France was worth far more than the gold plates reserved for less exalted guests lower down the pecking order.

When in the year 2000 the global Alcoa group, formerly the Aluminum Company of America, acquired an existing business in Birmingham at Kitts Green it not only bought a manufacturing facility but also acquired a sizeable chunk of local history.

Today Alcoa Europe's Kitts Green plant manufactures and sells aluminium alloy plate products and cast forging stock to the world's aerospace, defence, marine, transport and engineering markets. As Britain's largest aluminium plate mill Kitts Green competes internationally in all market sectors, exporting more than half its output. That output includes all the traditional aluminium alloys plus fascinating new developments such as low density aluminium-lithium aerospace alloys and the company's own range of specialist Alumec mould and tooling plate.

The plant at Kitts Green was built in 1938 by James Booth & Company; during the second world war it produced high strength aluminium alloys for aircraft and ships. But 1938 is far from being the start of our story, which has its origins in the middle of the 19th century.

Top: Making the propeller for the Schnieder plane, pictured are Berti Smith, Blacksmith and Billy Well, Manager. Right: Spitfire assembly at the works in Castle Bromwich. Above right: The Spitfire.

In 1869 two brothers, Edwin and James Grice, began working for themselves in a small way in Birmingham's Lower Fazeley Street. In 1872, needing capital to expand, they were joined by James Booth of Warwick. Under the name of Grice, Grice and Booth they acquired new premises in Sheepcote Street. There they installed rolling and drawing equipment enabling them to operate on a much larger scale, making brass and copper tubes for the chandelier and lamp trades.

Over the next decade the business prospered and the range of products expanded to include, brass tubes for stair rods, curtain rails, bedsteads and may similar items.

The partnership was dissolved following the death of Edwin Grice in 1882, leaving James Booth the sole proprietor. By 1892 James Booth and Company had acquired adjoining premises and laid out a new mill for the manufacture of bicycle

pumps and garden syringes, and, in a new material phosphor bronze, Bourdon Tubes for steam pressure gauges.

Near the end of the century Sheepcote Street was bursting at the seams. In 1898 James Booth bought the Kromand Metal Co Ltd and its Kromand Works in Argyle Street, Nechells. In 1901 the two businesses were amalgamated as James Booth & Company Ltd. Ten years later the events which would change the company's direction entirely began with an approach from Vickers.

In 1911 Vickers was looking for a manufacturer to produce its new lightweight 303 aluminium alloy cartridge cases made from 'Duralumin' and which were intended to reduce the weight of the bandoleers carried by infantrymen. Ironically as it would turn out in view of events still three years hence, Vickers had acquired the patent rights to Duralumin from a German company.

Germany the English patent rights to manufacture its Duralumin which had been discovered by Alfred Wilm, an employee of the German company, in 1908.

Wilm had been experimenting with an alloy of aluminium, copper and magnesium, and made the accidental observation that when this material was annealed - heated for some time - it first softened but after a few days got very much harder and stronger. Wilm realised that he had discovered a new phenomenon which he called 'age-hardening'. The essential requirement in a copper-aluminium alloy to cause age-hardening is the presence of magnesium, and this was the novel feature of the patent.

Subsequently Wilm found that he could double the strength of the alloy yet again by raising the temperature once more and then quickly bringing it down to room temperature by quenching the hot metal in water.

Vickers had initially become interested in Duralumin because it was looking at the possibility of airship production. As a consequence it had acquired from Durener Metallwerke of

Top: Electric Foundry Casting at Argyle Street in 1925.
Above: Casting Furnace, Argyle Street Works, 1936-38.

When Vickers bought the patent it had looked round for a means to investigate and exploit it, and thought that James Booth Ltd of Birmingham might be the ideal company to help.

By early 1914 considerable additions had been made to the rolling plant at Argyle Street and small quantities of Duralumin sheet were being produced, though with the exception of pioneer orders related to the airship industry, together with some small usage by the artificial limb industry, expected demand was small.

When war broke out later in 1914 the company concentrated all its production on munitions, mainly rolled brass plate for shells and cartridges. The following year however Vickers acquired the company and over the next four years invested heavily in the plant to produce Duralumin.

In the interwar years the development of aluminium alloys continued. Duralumin from Booths was used to build all but one of the historic 'R' series of British airships, though in terms of volume output as a proportion of the whole company Duralumin was still of negligible account. But in the mid 1930s that was about to change.

Airships were to prove a technological cul de sac, the future would belong to heavier than air flying machines, and they too would need lightweight alloys. The inventor Barnes Wallis had cut his teeth on airships and now applied his knowledge of Duralumin geodetic structures to the Wellington aeroplane with its robust basket like construction. As the Wellington bomber it would in a few years fly over enemy territory yet return again and again despite great holes shot through wings and fuselage.

Top: Continuous Casting machine at Kitts Green Foundry, 1942. ***Above:*** *Eric Welsh and Joe Billingsley examining the mast for HMS Ashant.*

Storm clouds gathered over Europe as the 1930s drew near their end. As the countdown to war began a completely new factory was built devoted entirely to the manufacture of aluminium alloy products, leaving the old Argyle Street premises to make copper-based products and magnesium alloys. Birmingham's then newest factory at Kitts Green, made its first delivery of Duralumin just days before the 1939-45 war broke out.

During the second world war thousands of tons of aluminium alloy in the form of sheet, strip, tube, extrusion, wire and forgings, including 200,000 propeller forgings, were delivered to the aircraft industry. Much larger tonnages of copper-based alloys products were delivered to the War Office and Admiralty. Winning the war on the 'Home Front' became as vital as that on the fighting front: the war would ultimately be won by the best supplied combatants.

As a safety measure another factory to shadow the forge in Birmingham was built by the company at Wrexham in North Wales well away from any industrial area. The shadow factory incorporated a 12,000 ton forging press with all the necessary amenities. Fortunately the Birmingham plant escaped enemy action, apart from 'the usual' incendiary bombs, and although Wrexham did produce small quantities of forgings it never came into full production and was disposed of after the war.

Left: *A 12 ton forging press installed at Mapplebeck's prior to the war.* **Below:** *The DC 3 pictured in 1962.*

Following the end of the war Booths continued to progress. During the war the company had been the first to install a truly continuous casting process which produced thousands of tons of aluminium alloy billets, mainly for the manufacture of aircraft spars for the later family of British bombers: the Lancaster, Stirling and Halifax.

A melting furnace and casting equipment far in advance of the competition were installed. Also installed was a '4-hi' hot mill 148" wide, the largest in Europe, to supply re-roll for the company's cold mills . This would be used to make foil stock and roll plates for ship building up to 12 feet wide, and thick plate for integral stringer section manufacture for aircraft.

In the late 1950s a British company, Delta Metal, acquired Booths. In 1959 Delta merged its aluminium interests with those of the Kaiser Aluminium Company of America. The Birmingham arm of this large corporation became James Booth Aluminium Ltd. The non-aluminium activities of the old business were absorbed into the rapidly expanding empire of the Delta Group whilst Kitts Green came mainly under the management wing of Delta's American partner, Kaiser Aluminium.

During the whole of the 1960s the Kitts Green factory witnessed a large programme of expansion.

Above: Preparations and foundation for the hot mill, 1960.
Below: Staff pictured outside the Foil Mill at Kitts Green.

By the mid 1960s the site capacity at Kitts Green was fully utilised. In 1964 the company took the decision to build a new factory at Skelmersdale in Lancashire. The Lancashire factory came into production in 1965, and would soon become the company's main light extrusion plant.

In the space vacated at Kitts Green by moving some plant to Skelmersdale an additional 64" high speed cold rolling mill was installed together with its ancillary furnaces. A cold tension levelling line was installed to provide fabricators with commercially flat sheet or coil.

As a result of additional investment, and a recovering world economy, during the 1960s the company increased its output

by 150 per cent. It also acquired its own solely owned distributor/warehousing facilities throughout the country, in addition to a fabricating company, a vehicle building company and close commercial associations with other outlets.

In 1966/67 the aluminium industry was subject of an investigation by the Prices & Incomes Board. In its report issued in August 1967 the Board stressed the over-capacity in the UK aluminium industry as well as the need to rationalise, to increase productivity and profitability.

The Prices & Incomes Board Report, coupled with a 1968 agreement to build smelters in the UK, led the Delta Metal Company to sell its 50 per cent holding in James Booth Aluminium. From December 1968 the company became owned half by the Kaiser Aluminium & Chemical Company and half by Alcan Industries Ltd. With the arrival of the 1970s the joint owners now began to trade as Alcan Booth Industries. Alcan subsequently increased its share holding to 75 pr cent, and by 1978 to 100 per cent, at which time the site changed its name to Alcan Plate.

A major investment was competed in 1982 with the installation of a horizontal heat treatment furnace.

More recently extensive investment has helped Kitts Green to become one of the leading manufacturers in the world of high technology plate in strong aluminium alloys. The Company supplies the aerospace, defence and engineering industries; customers are found throughout Europe, North and South America and the Far East.

Aerospace plate has been used to build such aircraft as Concorde, the Harrier jump jet, Jaguar and Tornado fighters,

*Top: Staff from Alcoa Kitts Green Foundry Department pictured with the Mayor and Mayoress after finishing their project at the Glebe Glitz, 2003. **Right:** Class A presentation to Alcoa, pictured are Andrew Perton and Ian McKinnon.*

as well as the European Airbus and various Boeing aircraft. Aluminium lithium forgings are used in the manufacture of the Westland Augusta EH101 helicopter.

Lightweight armour plate has even been supplied for armoured vehicles. Kitts Green's high strength heat treatable aluminium armour alloys form the entire hulls of both the Alvis Stormer and Warrior fighting vehicle families.

General engineering plate is used in moulds for the automotive industry as well as in many other applications not least at sea. Marine applications include fast ferries, cruise liners and leisure craft whilst land transport also includes railways and metro systems.

In 1996 Alcan sold the Kitts Green plant, together with 11 of its other 'down stream' businesses, to a consortium of investment fund holders to form a new company, British Aluminium Plate, in the process the new company became part of the Luxfer Group of companies.

In November 2000 British Aluminium Plate's Kitts Green site was sold, along with three other 'BAP' sites, to Alcoa, the world's largest aluminium company operating from over 400 locations in 38 countries and with more than 130,000 employees. Kitts Green became part of the Aerospace and General Engineering division within Alcoa Europe Flat Rolled Products.

Today Alcoa's Kitts Green plant with its sophisticated modern products has come a long way from the ornamental brass-cased iron bedstead tubes made by the Grice brothers back in the reign of Queen Victoria. The enterprise' story has been one of continuous development, enlargement, growth in knowledge and the ever extending application of that knowledge. But in some senses the story has never changed: it has been the story of exactly the same application, skill and devotion by generation after generation of

people who have produced success. In spite of all the fluctuations, peaks and slumps in our economy it has been the human factor which has mattered most. The history of Alcoa's Kitts Green plant demonstrates clearly what can be achieved with devoted and able staff backed by consistent investment in plant and ideas.

Image builders in print

'What good are thousands of copies of books when so few folk know how to read?' That's the question some pessimist must inevitably have asked Thomas Caxton when he introduced the first printing press to England in 1476. In theory the demand for printed works of all kinds from books to advertising leaflets should have been small in a world where the literate formed just a small minority of the population: in reality the demand for the printed word was, and remains, insatiable.

Birmingham's own successor to Thomas Caxton is Louis Drapkin Ltd. The family firm may not be able to trace its origins back to the 15th century, but it certainly goes back far longer than most.

Amongst the many Midlands' success stories, Louis Drapkin Ltd must rank as one of the most progressive of family-owned printing businesses in the city of Birmingham. From moderate beginnings as a general jobbing printer in 1937, the company has overcome wartime bombing raids, industry set-backs, national recessions and fierce competition to become, today, one of the leading printing houses in the city.

The company history begins with its founder, Louis Drapkin, who served his trade apprenticeship with V. Siviter Smith &

Top: Founder, Mr Louis Drapkin. **Below:** *A 1960s Heidelberg Double Crown printing press used for cutting and creasing.*

Co, a well-known Midland block-making firm. Louis went on to gain considerable experience with other processing houses before entering into a partnership in 1936 with a practical printer, Mr P Horton. Together they opened for business as Drapkin Horton in Newtown Row and work soon began to pour in. Before long they were forced to re-locate to bigger premises in Birmingham's Newhall Street. Although the work load continued to expand, the partnership was brought to an end by mutual agreement, and in 1937 a new company, Louis Drapkin Ltd, set out on its own from premises in Fleet Street, off Summer Row.

Despite both Britain and world's economy being in the midst of the Depression the closing years of 'hungry thirties' were nevertheless a time of optimism for the young printer embarking for the first time on a business venture entirely on his own. Had Louis Drapkin realised that another world war lay around just around the corner he might however have been rather less optimistic.

At the outbreak of war with Nazi Germany in September 1939 the firm re-located to Wrottesley Street. With modest plant, comprising two Heidelberg platen machines, as well as a Crown polymatic cylinder and a 32 in Perfecta guillotine, Louis Drapkin wasted little time in making his mark as a successful businessman. Within just 12 months, despite wartime restrictions, he had recorded a turnover of £5,000.

Overcoming wartime difficulties, which brought constant interruptions through bombing, labour shortages and limited supply of materials, the company managed to continue as it began despite the nightly threats posed by Hitler's Luftwaffe. In such desperate times however Louis' luck could not last for ever. Trade remained brisk, until, in October 1943 disaster struck and Louis Drapkin lost his factory in an enemy bombing raid.

Louis Drapkin however, was not the sort of man to allow a minor set back like having his premises blown to smithereens put him out of business. Salvaging as much of the plant as he could, Louis took temporary residence in a converted car showroom in Wellington Road, Perry Barr. The next two years were physically demanding to say the least. When he was not carrying out his three nights a week air raid warden duties in Selly Oak, Louis spent every other evening fire-watching on the other side of the city at his premises in Perry Barr. This was in addition to his demanding workload during the day. Nevertheless, under Louis' direction, the firm's turnover continued to grow.

By 1948 the level of business forced another move for Louis Drapkin Ltd, this time to the site of a former public house in Lawley Street, Birmingham. Shortly after, in anticipation

Top: The Machine Room and Warehouse in the 1960s.

of even further expansion, the firm commissioned a new, purpose-built premises in Allcock Street, Digbeth, comprising a double bay factory and single-storey office block.

Building work was completed in 1954 and the company moved in during the summer of that year, occupying only a quarter of the floor space when the plant was finally installed. But, as business continued to prosper and new plant was brought in, it wasn't long before the newly appointed Managing Director Keith Drapkin was advising his father on further expansion plans to secure the company's long term future.

In 1960 a second storey was built over the office block to accommodate the increase in staff. Seven years later the company was again bursting at the seams and the car park had to give way to provide an extra 1,500 sq ft of offices, warehousing and a loading area.

When the premises next door became vacant in 1971, Louis Drapkin took the opportunity to expand, using the extra 4,000 sq ft of floor space to house the company's own graphics studio and litho plate-making operation. Brian Draper was brought in to manage the new venture and eventually went on become the company's Managing Director.

The new acquisition also enabled changes to be made to the factory layout and heralded, a then ambitious £50,000, investment programme in printing machinery and equipment to help consolidate the company's position both in the litho and

letterpress printing markets. New plant included a Heidelberg Sorkz high-speed litho machine capable of turning out 10,000 two-colour printed sheets an hour, and a bank of the latest cylinder and platen machines.

As the company grew, so the business has changed, from that of a general jobbing printer to a highly respected, high-quality four-colour specialist printer. The early 1970s saw the demise of traditional letterpress printing methods. New technology and the super-fast litho process were now having a significant influence on the printing industry.

Top: The Platen Department, mid 1960s.
Above: Staff gather for the presentation to Arthur Burns for 50 years service at Louis Drapkin, May 1991.

are especially proud of their vintage 1966 Heidelberg cylinder press that sits happily amongst the gleaming new print room equipment. Today, it still performs a valuable job cutting and creasing printed sheets with the same accuracy as it did the day it was first installed. The talented workforce also has a habit of staying around, adding to Drapkin's enviable reputation for maintaining a well below average staff turnover. Towards the end of 2004, no fewer than five dedicated employees were each celebrating 25 years of service with the company.

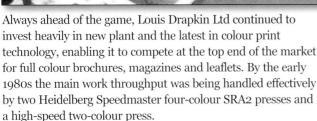

Always ahead of the game, Louis Drapkin Ltd continued to invest heavily in new plant and the latest in colour print technology, enabling it to compete at the top end of the market for full colour brochures, magazines and leaflets. By the early 1980s the main work throughput was being handled effectively by two Heidelberg Speedmaster four-colour SRA2 presses and a high-speed two-colour press.

The volume of work increased in proportion to the demands of a growing portfolio of clients throughout the country in general, as well as in the Midlands.

Higher quality levels, better cost efficiency and speed of delivery were the driving forces behind an on-going investment programme. In the mid 1990s the Heidelberg presses gave way to even faster, more efficient Mitsubishi four-colour machines. These have now been replaced by a five-colour Mitsubishi machine with a coating facility, capable of handling huge volumes of work in Drapkin's busy round-the-clock working schedule.

Plate-making is still handled in-house but now benefits from the latest in computer-to-plate (CTP) technology, introduced for the new millennium and now upgraded to the latest in industry standards. The process dispenses with the need for intermediate film separations, delivering high-quality printing plates direct to the press together with computerised colour balance machine codes and make-ready instructions.

To maintain greater control of quality and subsequent costs, much of the finishing work that was once out-sourced is now carried out in-house. From plate-making to printing, to collating, binding and lamination, Louis Drapkin Ltd now has the equipment and capability to see the job through from start to finish, however large or small.

But while plant and machinery have to move with the times, some printers are determined to stand their ground. Drapkin's

Ever-challenging customer demands will continue to influence new developments in both print technology and production. For Louis Drapkin Ltd this will mean further investment in plant, machinery and personnel. Soon the future of the company will be the responsibility of Keith Drapkin's son, Joel, the third generation of the Drapkin family, destined to take forward a proud heritage founded on the printing needs of Birmingham's industrial post-war development.

Top left: *The Machine Room in 1991.*
Top right: *A five colour B1 Mitsubishi Printing Press with coating unit.* **Below:** *Company Directors, 2004, from left to right: Joel Drapkin, Keith Drapkin and Brian Draper.*

Salts of the earth

Today Birmingham's Salts Healthcare, based in Lord Street, Nechells, specialises in manufacturing and distributing ostomy supplies and 'orthotics' or orthopaedic appliances. But the company has come an awful long way from its roots in the 18th century.

Salts Healthcare is one of the oldest 'family run' businesses in the country. The Salt family can trace its origins back to the early 1700s when two brothers, John and William Salt, were apprenticed to locksmiths in Wolverhampton.

John Salt subsequently made and repaired knives, saddles, plough shares, shoes and anything else which required skilled work involving leather and metal. By the time of his death in 1755 however, John Salt was firmly established as a 'Surgeons Instrument Maker' and Cutler. The business was taken over by John's son William who, after learning the family trade in London, was a journeyman for a Mr La Roche in Silver Street near to Golden Square.

William Salt appears to have been a typical Midlands metal worker of the period; he appears in the Wolverhampton Directory of 1770 as a cutler, and is listed in the Birmingham Directory of 1780 as a 'toyman'. Though Salts continued making surgical instruments clearly they also traded in other wares.

The 1783 medical register for Staffordshire and Warwickshire lists 82 medical practitioners, many of whom were no doubt supplied with instruments made by Salts. Since surgeons replaced their instruments only infrequently however, Salts' needed to also develop other business as cutlers and toy makers. Happily new medical advances required old instruments to be updated, and new instruments to be developed, ensuring a steady trade for Salts.

Above: Sir Edward Salt, Conservative MP for Yardley 1931-1946 and High Sheriff of Warwickshire in the 1950s.
Below: Testing artificial limbs at Uffculme Hospital in 1923.

William Salt died in 1793 and the firm passed to Richard Salt who moved the business to new premises in Dale End, Birmingham in the early 1800s.

The firm prospered in this period and Richard, still specialising in making surgical instruments, opened additional premises in Coleshill Street. After his death Richard's wife ran the business for some time; this was unusual at that time, and in due course the firm passed to Richard's son Thomas Partridge Salt.

Thomas Partridge Salt died during the cholera epidemic of 1840-41 at the age of 45. His widow Mary and their son however kept the business going. In 1845 they moved to bigger and more prestigious premises in Bull Street.

The pace now quickened. The national economy was improving. The third quarter of the 19th century saw trade in Birmingham pick up, bringing with it even greater prosperity for Salts. Whilst continuing as surgical instrument makers and truss manufacturers, in 1854 Salts attained a new and exalted status as 'Cutlers to Her Majesty'.

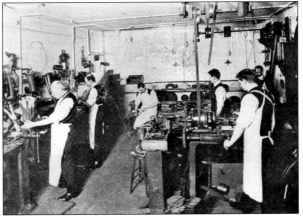

In 1863 Salts was granted a Royal Warrant, and in 1867 also became Cutlers to the Emperor of the French.

Salts was one of 57 exhibitors at the 1867 Paris Universal Exhibition and was awarded an 'Honourable mention'. A key figure in Salts' success at that time was the second TP Salt. In 1845 the firm had changed its name to Salt M & Son but by 1867 it had changed again to Salt & Son.

The second TP Salt had become influential in local matters in the 1850s. TP Salt was also at the forefront in his specialist field. In 1865 TP Salt published 'On Rupture: Its Causes, Management and Cure, and Various Mechanical Contrivances Employed for its Relief'. In 1866 he published 'A Treatise on Deformities and Debilities of the Lower extremities'. The frontispiece features a General Knolley presenting his compliments and commenting that the work is a 'valuable contribution to Science'. There is an original copy of this work in the Birmingham Library.

Top: One of Salt & Son Ltd's early fitting rooms.
Above : Early artificial limbs.
Left: Artificial Limb Making.

In addition to his own writing TP Salt also subscribed to the production of JA Langford's 'A century of Birmingham Life 1741-1841' published in 1868.

TP Salt obviously enjoyed his work and took a very active interest in the business. A case book of the period reveals that he attended to a diverse range of conditions from amputations to back complaints. Patients were also being seen by Ashton T Salt the great, great grandfather of the Salt brothers who currently run the firm.

The economic depression of the mid 1860s did not appear to affect Salts, which by then were describing themselves as 'Surgical Instrument Makers and Anatomical Mechanicians to the Prince of Wales.

Salts patented its 'Orthonemic' Truss in this period. Keen Europeans even then, the firm exhibited at the 1876 Brussels International Exhibition, giving prominence to its 'trusses and other new inventions in aid of medicine and surgery'. In this last quarter of the 19th century the firm began to concentrate on medical products and dropped cutlery making.

TP Salt had led the firm from Birmingham's Bull Street in 1863, moving it to Corporation Street before relocating to Cherry Street in 1900.

The demand for medical products grew throughout the first half of the 20th century. This was partly due to increasing innovation in the field of medical science. But equally this increase in demand was also due to the millions of injuries sustained by servicemen during the Great War of 1914-18.

The second world war which broke out in 1939 would act as a similar spur to development in many areas of healthcare. The year 1941 found Salts concentrating on artificial limb production, but the focus changed in 1945 when contracts for artificial limb makers were reassessed on the cessation of hostilities and in the run up to the creation of the National Health Service in 1948.

In 1948 Professor Brian Brooke returned from the USA full of enthusiasm for the work the Americans were doing with Ileostomy patients. Professor Brooke asked Salts if it could make bowel contents collection devices which could be

Top: Leather covering and belt making.
Above: Early crutches.

tered by patients. The advice is made available in a variety of settings, including in patients' own homes.

The Orthotics Division at Salts provides manufacturing, measuring and a fitting service for orthopaedic appliances to NHS and private hospitals. The measuring and fitting is carried out by Salts' team of qualified orthotists working within the hospital as part of an orthopaedic consultant's team.

A Distribution Division provides specialist home delivery of ostomy, incontinence, orthopaedic and surgical products to hospitals, wholesalers and retail chemists.

Meanwhile the company's export policy is to work with specially selected distributors in overseas countries providing the sales and marketing back up needed by them to achieve significant market penetration.

attached to the abdomen similar to those being produced in the USA.

An approach by EA St J 'Ted' Salt for a supply or licensing agreement proved fruitless, so Salts did some basic development work of its own and went ahead with a limited range of 'handmade' Ileostomy pouches.

Over the following years Salts continued to improve the pouches, and although it was provided as a free of charge service, the firm was delighted to be able to radically improve the lifestyle of stoma patients. This would however eventually lead to a whole range of Salts stoma care products.

In 1996 Salt & Son Ltd acquired the business of Eurocare and its factory based in Horsham, West Sussex. The acquisition strengthened Salts' position in both the United Kingdom and the overseas ostomy market. A highly specialised team is now based in Horsham designing , developing and producing Salts innovative range of ostomy products.

Salts Patient Care Division provides specialist advice to product users and professionals. Ostomy, incontinence and wound care can all benefit directly and indirectly from Salt's qualified team of nurses and product advisers. The Salts Patient Care Service is provided free of charge to both hospitals and patients.

An Ostomy Care Service provided by Salts includes expert advice on the selection and use of appropriate products from a range of manufacturers, as well as offering advice on dealing with the inevitable problems encoun-

Today Salts, now trading as Salts Healthcare Ltd, is a leading manufacturer and supplier of healthcare products; it provides a truly international service in a global marketplace, whilst still retaining the traditional values that only a highly personal service can offer.

John Salt, starting out in business for himself in the 18th century, could surely never for one moment have envisaged that 300 years later that not only would his firm have survived the centuries, but that his family name would now be familiar to clients across the globe.

Top left: Philip Salt greets Claire Short MP for Ladywood to Salts Healthcare for a Factory Visit, 2003. ***Below:*** The Salt Family.

On the move

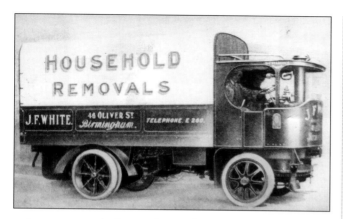

are too many over confident 'chimps' who rick backs, scratch antiques and strain marriages trying to do it themselves. Why use professionals to do the selling, buying and legal work and then trust an amateur with your most valued possessions? This is where a company such as White's comes into its own. This is no Johnny come lately business. In 1998, it celebrated its centenary. Over a century of experience isn't to be sneezed at. How many thousands of armchairs have been moved, how many millions of books have been carried and how many cups of tea drunk in that time? It hardly bears thinking about. Yet, it is that very experience that inspires confidence. With it comes the gratitude of satisfied customers who provide the best advert any company can get - personal recommendation. There have been plenty of those since those late Victorian days.

'**D**ad, do you know the piano's on my foot?' 'You hum it son and I'll play it!' No-one who saw the televised tea adverts featuring the PG Chimps will ever forget that hilarious line as the chimps from a removal firm attempted to manoeuvre a piano down a flight of stairs.

But although that bit of light hearted entertainment still amuses us we certainly wouldn't want to have set of chimps getting hold of our valued possessions when we decide to move. Happily here in Birmingham we have the chance to use the services of one of the country's most experienced removal companies: Whites Removals and Transport Ltd.

The most trying of times for families are said to be divorce, death and moving. By the time the divorce court looms it is often too late to do anything other than accept the situation. There's not much we can do about dying, either. When you've got to go, you've got to go. But moving house is another matter. It may be another case of having no choice about going, but you do have some control. Having found your new home and a solicitor to sort out the legal work, all that remains is to book a reliable company to move your belongings. It is no good trying to do it yourself. There

The company's founder, JF White, was no novice when it came to dealing with the public and moving their house contents from one home to another; he had already worked in the removal trade before trying his luck on his own. But it was a big step to go it alone, and there were times when he wondered whether or not he had done the right thing. However, with the perseverance of the Victorian, he was determined to succeed.

Mr White was a familiar sight working in and around the Birmingham area, leaving the yard of 35 Cromwell Street, Nechells to start his day moving some excited family on its way to a new challenge and adventure. The transport was, of course, provided in those times by one horse-drawn dray. Removals might have meant more than one journey for both man and beast. Hail, rain or shine would find Mr White behind a pair of sturdy Shires, his feet on the dashboard calling to his

*Top left: Whites original steam driven removal lorry. **Right:** The original horse drawn vehicle.*

charges and flicking their reins. How would he have regarded the air-conditioned cabins and smooth ride of the vehicles of today? Would he have thought of them as a luxury or turned up his nose at the soft living of the modern removal man? All we can say is that the employees of our times would not trade places for a gold clock.

Ironically White's itself has never moved very far despite being in the removal business. It has continued to operate from Nechells throughout its entire existence. The premises have changed, but the locality has not. Consequently, a steady client base has been established and families have come back to White's, 'the removal people' time and again to use the service they know they can rely on. After Cromwell Street, it was on Oliver Street that the business continued to prosper. The current base is to be found at 257 Great Lister Street. It is only here that one can really appreciate the size of the enterprise. When the company came to these premises in the 1950s it occupied 8,000 sq ft. Now there are no fewer than 31,000 sq ft of space. Every inch is fully utilised. It is certainly a far cry from the days of the dray. These days huge vans sweep along the motorways across the length and breadth of Britain. And it is not just this country that sees them, either. White's is a truly international operation. If you stick a pin anywhere on the globe it is almost certain that White's Removals and Transport has arranged to convey some house

Top: Whites premises in Oliver Street.
Above left: A White's removal lorry pictured whilst moving the Birmingham Symphony Orchestra.

bankrupt stock will wonder what to do with it whilst the creditors' meetings are continuing and the premises sealed. Send for White's! Even the ordinary householder wanting to store possessions whilst moving out of one house and waiting for the next one to be ready knows the answer: White's.

contents, office furniture or other goods to that destination. The firm is particularly well known in South Africa, India and Australia.

In addition to the familiar house moves White's is also heavily involved in the removal and storage of archives and files. Solicitors often use the company's services for this purpose. Sitting in a small legal office somewhere in the city centre, a solicitor's clerk will be looking at a pile of ancient documents that are no use to anyone. Collecting dust, they are using space that could be freed for better use. The answer? Send for White's. Accountants anguishing over a load of

Top left: Moving the Sutton Coalfield News in the late 1950s. Top right: Bill Kitchen (seated) and sons Nigel (left) and Richard pictured in 1978. Below: Whites 1950s premises.

At White's base storage is provided in containerised units. Clients can feel secure in the knowledge that everything is under lock and key in the repository. Not only that, the temperature is fixed and there are no worries about damp or damage from the elements. There would be nothing worse than digging out Aunty's old will, in which she had intended to leave you her jewels, only to find that the paper had disintegrated. No chance of that in a dedicated container. Your inheritance is in safe hands.

One of the golden rules of the business is that care must always been taken of other people's property. No job was ever too small to be skimped. At one time delicate porcelain was moved in a special contraption called a china van. The floor was removed and the breakables stored below. Furniture was then piled onto the replaced flooring.

White's has handled some of the largest jobs imaginable. In the 1980s, the contents of Aston Hall were removed to store whilst it was being refurbished. Special crates were made. Marble tables, 47 works of art, countless ornaments and all the furniture were taken to headquarters in the high security warehouse.

The cornerstone of White's business throughout the 20th century and now into the 21st has been its reliable

by the end of this new century. So successful has the firm been that you would not bet against it. What price for a container service to Mars in the 22nd century? Technology has moved us from the horse-drawn dray to the steam-driven vans and right through to transporting across continents. Nothing would surprise us today, though such thoughts though would surely have been far from the mind of the driver of White's old steam driven lorry: he had to get up at four o'clock in order to raise enough pressure in the boiler for an eight o'clock start.

Meanwhile, with so much experience behind White's Removals and Transport, it's almost sad to relate that the one thing you won't ever hear from them are those immortal words 'Dad, do you know the piano's on my foot'!

and trouble free service. It is the way that the family business has always operated, and it intends to do so for another 100 years. There have now been five generations of the family involved in the running of the company. After the founder came EJ White, followed by Bill Kitchen and his sons Richard and Nigel. The fifth and, most certainly, not the last are Jamie and Sam. They are on hand to take the firm on in the new millennium. Who knows; perhaps there will be White's vans on a space shuttle to the moon

*Above: A Whites horse drawn china van participating in the Birmingham Horse Parade. **Below:** 1983 and Whites are parked up ready to start the removal of contents from the Aston Hall as it undergoes refurbishment. **Right:** One of White's fleet in 2004.*

On the ball

Londoners may know a thing or two about great engineering projects, but when problems occurred with the new Millennium footbridge over the Thames they turned to a Birmingham firm to help provide the solution to stop that prestige project from swinging in the breeze.

Alwayse Engineering supplied 68 specially designed stainless steel ball transfer units which work with the viscous dampers which have been added to the bridge by engineering consultants Arup and fitted by the Cleveland Bridge Company.

A prototype ball transfer unit was tested extensively by Arup for more than 56 million cycles, then subjected to a thousand hours of salt spray for corrosion followed by a further 11 million cycles before finally being put to use on the bridge. Seated in hardened steel plates the units have to be made completely from stainless steel because of the highly corrosive environment they operate in.

Moving heavy objects in the long ago past was undoubtedly something of a black art. In far away Egypt just how did the Egyptians move the enormous blocks of stone to build those wonders of the ancient world, the pyramids?

And nearer to home what about Stonehenge? It would surely have taken something more than four brawny men, one at each corner, to shift the great monoliths which make up that prehistoric monument. Put them on a cart would be an obvious answer; or it would be, were it not for the fact that any of the stones which make up that mighty circle would crush the strongest wheels and snap the thickest axles.

The answer to our ancestors' problem is that after a river journey the huge stones could be moved overland by dragging them over solid rollers made from tree trunks. Today's answer to similar problems is the ball bearing.

Ball bearings provide almost frictionless contact between moving parts. Without them engines would seize up within minutes. Younger readers may have been puzzled by why during the second world war the German

Luftwaffe made such strenuous attempts to destroy such seemingly mundane targets as Britain's ball bearing factories - or indeed why the RAF should be prepared to sacrifice so many bombers and their crews on similar missions in the skies over Germany. The reason of course is that although they are tiny, ball bearings were a large part of each country's war machines - both literally and figuratively. Without their ball bearings, planes, tanks, lorries and ships were simply useless lumps of metal.

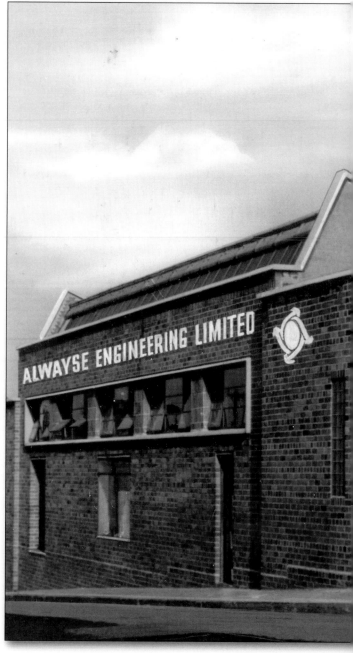

Right: Alwayse Engineering Limited's Warner Street Premises in the late 1960s.

Mr A Pinnick was a furniture retailer with a large shop in Birmingham. He purchased a small engineering company, in 1939, called Sheridan Precision Tool Co., which would become the seed of today's internationally renowned Alwayse Engineering Ltd. This company had previously been owned by a Walter William Wise, who was a mildly eccentric inventor, always wearing a dark suit, winged collar, Pince-nez glasses and what for those days was considered to be long hair. It was his idea to mount a large ball in a cup of small balls in order to allow the load ball to move in all directions.

During the second world war the company at first made ammunition boxes. After receiving new machinery under the American lend lease arrangement it was commended on several occasions for producing quite intricate work, and prototype parts, for gas turbine engines.

In 1945 at the end of hostilities it was necessary to find new products; one idea, derived from Mr Pinnick's furniture background, was to produce castors.

Possibly the idea came to him from the carved 'ball and claw' wooden feet which had been a feature of furniture for centuries. Based on this invention the Company renamed itself Alwayse, to indicate that the unit could move in all directions.

Unhappily there were problems for the new castor being used on furniture. At the end of the war Mr Leon Pinnick, the company's present Chairman, left college and joined Alwayse. He saw the potential for turning the ball unit the opposite way up to a castor, and of building it into equipment for the material handling industry.

Now the company began to manufacture what it called an industrial 'Ball Transfer Unit'.

There began a gradual development towards the design and manufacture of purpose-built ball units for specific applications. A further natural progression was to produce related equipment such as Ball Transfer Tables, platforms, and later Air Cargo Ball Mats and decks.

In those early days the company also produced its own low grade solid steel balls. Subsequently however these would be bought in.

Instead Alwayse began to manufacture hollow steel balls of one inch and one and 9/16ths diameter. The hollow balls originally arose from a requirement from Short Brothers and Harland in Belfast who were probably the first aircraft manufacturers to install hollow steel balls inside the cargo decks of aircraft. The advantage of being hollow meant a major saving in weight.

In 1969 the company moved to its current premises in Warner Street, together with its sister company the Alwayse Castor Co Ltd. Here Ball transfer Units were manufactured by Alwayes Engineering Ltd, alongside the Alwayse Castor company which was a stockist of wheels and castors.

Alwayse Engineering is now the largest manufacturer of ball transfer units in the world. The company exports to over 60 countries, with more than two thirds of output being sold abroad. More than 140 different models are made with load capacities from 6 kilograms to 4,000.

In 1983 Zoe Lawton, Leon Pinnick's daughter joined Alwayse Castors to help continue the company's inexorable drive forward. She and her husband Peter Lawton are directors of both companies. Alwayse Engineering is headed by their Managing Director Graham Golby who has been with the company since 1991, during which time the annual turnover has tripled.

The company has a wide and diverse customer list that includes such well known names as Australian Defence Industries, the Bank of England, British Aerospace, British Airways, Dunlop, Electrolux, FMC Airline Equipment, Jaguar Cars, Levi Strauss & Co, Lodige,

Top: Early company catalogues.
Right: Alwayse Engineering supplied 110,000 Ball Transfer Units for Continental Airlines' terminal at Newark International Airport.

35 years - despite being in his late seventies he remains extremely active, maintaining the company's power presses. Another 14 people have been whom Alwayes for more than a decade, four of whom have clocked up a quarter of a century.

Expansion into adjacent premises in Warwick Street and an extension built in 1998 testify to its continued growth, with plans for a move to larger purpose built premises in on a two acre site in Aston now in the pipeline.

Meanwhile, if any Birmingham folk visiting London and taking a stroll over that Millennium Bridge might like to take a closer look at its construction. The Alwayse ball units, each with a load ball diameter of 50 mm and a load capacity of 1330 kg, are attached to the ends of the new chevron steelwork which can be clearly seen from the underside of the bridge. Those chevrons hold the viscous dampers. When there is any twist in the bridge the dampers absorb any large movement whilst the ball units from Alwayse Engineering take up the small oscillations left from them.

There's no doubt that this is one Birmingham company at least which is indisputably 'on the ball'!

Lotus Cars Ltd, Philips Worldwide, Plessey Systems, Rockwell Fletcher, Rolls Royce, SKF USA/Canada and Windoff.

Alwayse has enjoyed many successes over the years, but one of its most recent has been at the new Hong Kong International Airport where the company's ball units are the only make installed in the various Air Cargo locations

Rewards comes in many forms: in 1997 however the company received one of industry's highest accolades, when it became a recipient of the Queen's Award for Export Achievement.

Having once employed only three people, today Alwayse Engineering employs a workforce of more than 50. The company enjoys and enviable reputation for retaining its staff: the longest serving member of which is Ray Jeffs who has been with the business for

Top left: An Alwayse promotional stand.
Left: Examples of Alwayse Die Tables.
Below: An artists impression of Alwayse Engineering Limited's new state-of-the-art factory. At 44,000sq ft and designed and built specifically to the company's requirements for manufacturing Ball Transfer Units not only will it give ample space for today's requirements, but will also give the company adequate capacity for future expansion.

Forged in fire

One of the West Midlands' best known exports is comedian Lenny Henry. But if Lenny hadn't taken the high road to international success then exactly where in the city might he have worked?

In the 1980s that question was puzzling BBC producers. As a result of their head scratching a Birmingham manufacturing company received a visit from the BBC. The visitors were producing the Lenny Henry Show which was to feature one programme with an episode set in a factory where Lenny's character had come to work. With the company's agreement a large team of programme makers arrived at the factory one morning - and all for the sake of two minutes worth of programming!

The company chosen by the BBC was Rainsford & Lynes Ltd. The firm may not have been the recipient of quite all of Andy Warhol's promised fifteen minutes of televisual fame, but having already been around for more than a century the company was already known in the area.

Today Birmingham's Rainsford & Lynes Ltd specialises in the production of machined hot brass forgings used by a wide variety of industries from central heating boiler manufacturers, to diesel engines and shower units. A significant proportion of production goes to Rainsford & Lynes' sister company Bullfinch (Gas Equipment) Ltd.

Both Rainsford & Lynes and Bullfinch can trace their origins to William Lynes who was born in 1859. In 1879 at the age of 20, having learned the trade of brass founding, he formed a partnership with his Uncle, a Mr Vincent.

Top left: *William Lynes, founder of Rainsford & Lynes.*
Below: *The Tool Room in the 1960s.*

Thomas Rainsford died in 1928. The Rainsford family had been important to the business through the capital they had injected into it; their interest in the firm however came to an end with the death of Thomas.

At the end of the first world war Stanley and Robert Lynes had joined their father in the business. In 1921 they pioneered the use of hot brass stampings for brass fittings, becoming one of the first companies in the Midlands to install hot stamping presses. Although the company continued to make castings until after the second world war these would be gradually phased out in favour of stampings.

Stanley Lynes became a Director in 1930. Stanley and Robert Lynes would go on to jointly manage the company following their father's death in 1934.

Together they produced gas fittings from brass castings at premises in Dymoke Street, Highgate, Birmingham.

The business and its product range expanded rapidly and the firm soon moved to larger premises, just around the corner in Emily Street, where it would remain until 1962.

After the death of his uncle, William Lynes formed a new partnership, this time with Thomas Rainsford, a member of a well known Birmingham family. The new partnership became a limited company in 1896.

In the years just before the second world war the situation at Rainsford & Lynes, along with many other Birmingham companies, was very difficult because of the lack of work. A post war boom period of the early 1920s had given way to economic recession. The Wall Street Crash of 1929 would be

Top: The assembly of Bullfinch products, 1960s.
Above left: Comedian Lenny Henry and the BBC use the Rainsford & Lynes factory to shoot a scene for Lenny Henry's character as a factory worker.

the start of something far worse: a full scale world wide depression of trade. Soon millions were on the dole. Stan Lynes himself, even though he was Managing Director, was at times found working on the factory floor helping with production in order to keep costs down. The run up to the second world war however, sad though it is to say, did eventually bring in more work.

But, though the company may have made progress during the war, the post war years held a nasty surprise of their own. In the 1950s there was severe fire at the Emily Street premises: at the time this seemed like a disaster but on the plus side it did at least mean that the company was able to re-equip parts of the factory with new equipment.

The 1950s were to prove a decade of change. Following the acquisition of a patent taken out by two engineers, Messrs Ball and Finch, for a blow torch working off towns gas, Rainsford & Lynes produced towns gas torches for some years before it was found that LP gas (Liquefied Petroleum Gas - sold commercially as propane and butane) was a better fuel for that kind of application. The company developed new torches which worked off LPG. Bullfinch (Gas Equipment) Ltd came into existence as a separate company in 1959; its success and the rapid expansion of its product range in the mid 1960s necessitated the move of many of its functions to a former bakery in Shipway Road, Hay Mills, Birmingham which would eventually be redeveloped into a separate modern factory built in 1974. Management and sales however continued to be based at Kings Road.

In 1962 the redevelopment of the Highgate area meant that Rainsford & Lynes had to find new premises. A move was made to 35,000 square feet premises all on one level: to the present premises, the Diadem Works at Kings Road, Tyseley.

Stanley Lynes (Mr Will to the employees) had retired as Managing Director in 1950, though he remained as Chairman until his death in 1973. His brother Robert Lynes (Mr Bob to the staff) was sole Managing Director from 1950 until his death in 1968.

Bob Lynes was a flamboyant character who had the vision to develop Bullfinch and guide the company to what it is today; he was always interested in the latest technology - as well as in the high life: in the later stages of his control of the company his interest in the latter included running a Rolls Royce car! Under his guidance staff numbers had grown to around 130.

On Bob Lynes' death Graham Williams, his and Stanley's nephew who had already been with the company since 1934, took over, and in 1973 he was joined by Andrew Williams, great grandson of founder William Lynes, who became a Director in 1976.

Top right: *Managing Director Graham Williams with Works Manager Norman Roby in the 1970s, Bullfinch heaters can be seen behind.* ***Above:*** *Graham Williams with George and Nellie Turner at the company's centenary celebration in 1979 as between them the Turners had over one hundred years service.*

By the time of its centenary in 1979 Rainsford & Lynes was involved in the production of machined hot brass stampings and assemblies and turned parts made from brass bar which were used by the gas, electrical, water, refrigeration and general engineering industries, as well as supplying its associate company Bullfinch.

Twenty years after it had come into existence Bullfinch was designing, manufacturing and marketing blowtorches, lights, heaters, furnaces, regulators and fittings for LP gas and had become acknowledged as one of the United Kingdom's leading manufacturers of its range of equipment.

In the following decades Bullfinch has been at the forefront of equipment design, introducing new features such as spark ignition into torches, heaters and lights. At one stage the company even manufactured gas powered traffic lights - though perhaps unsurprisingly the formidable technical problems led to the product being withdrawn!

Over the years Rainsford & Lynes has brought in many new methods of manufacture, from brass forging presses at the beginning of the last century to rotary transfer machines in the middle decades of the century. Today the challenge is to find flexible low cost automation, making it possible for the company to compete with manufacturers operating in low wage cost economies overseas. As a result of investment staff numbers have been reduced in recent years from the peak of 130 in the 1970s to around 80 today.

Rainsford & Lynes is continuously improving techniques, and driving down unit costs by the use of computers, automation, computer controlled machine tools, and in modern quality management systems. Both companies have been dependant on the loyalty and skill of their work forces. The challenge for the future is to continue to innovate and to use these skills more efficiently.

Bullfinch meanwhile has moved into producing torches that work well on small cylinders of gas; it is also now distributing other products from both UK and around the world. A depot has been opened in Essex to provide space to stock those products and to help provide an improved service to the South east of England.

Though most sales are within the United Kingdom a significant proportion of the output of both Bullfinch and Rainsford & Lynes output now goes to export.

Graham Williams died in April 2004. Following semi-retirement in 1985 he had continued as Chairman, still spending half a day each week working in the business. His son, Andrew Williams, had already become Managing Director on Graham's retirement and is now leading the two sister companies in the 21st century.

Top left: Rainsford & Lynes' old Emily Street premises in 1900.
Top right: Rainsford & Lynes' premises, 2004.
Left: Production using modern CNC machinery.

Keeping the heat in

Shadwell House, in Shadwell Street, a location at the white hot heart of Birmingham's old gun quarter, is the home of a business which for more than half a century has been at the forefront of making sure that all the heat generated by industry stays exactly where it was supposed to be.

What is now the FGF Organisation, made up of a group of companies, specialising in supplying industry both at home and abroad with fire protection materials, dry lining, cladding and all types of insulation.

The range of goods on offer to customers is astonishing: roofing sheets, plastering and dry lining; ventilation products, damp proof courses; floor, wall, roof and loft insulation; glass and ceramic textiles, pipe, duct and mattress insulation, ceramic fibres and refractory materials such as such as firebricks and fire cement.

In addition to supplying manufacturers' standard sizes, this multi million pound business also offers its clients a comprehensive cutting and machining service from local depots across the country. With its additional facilities for facing and fabrication FGF offers the ideal tailor-made service to the construction and engineering industries.

The creation of FGF, this remarkable business, can be traced to the vision of one man - still going strong though now in his eighties - its Chairman and founder FS Mayman, who established the firm in the early 1950s.

Asbestos had been discovered in South Africa and Canada in the latter part of the 19th century.

Above: Founder, FS Mayman.
Below: FGF's premises on Princip Street corner, circa 1974.

British industry immediately realised the tremendous potential of the mineral which was not only fire and heat proof but could be woven like any other fibre. The first consignment of asbestos arrived in Birmingham around 1880 and was eagerly seized upon. Whilst factories in Lancashire began spinning asbestos yarn others experimented with creating asbestos boards, pipes and lagging.

Asbestos proved to be the ideal material for a vast range of industrial applications wherever heat and fire were present. Manufacturers would develop many more asbestos products such as packing, fibre joints, millboard and paper.

The early origins of FGF however don't go back quite as far as the 1880s, but they can be traced back almost as far as the first world war.

FS Mayman's introduction to the world of business came through a company founded by his father in 1920: the Birmingham firm of King, Mayman and King, manufacturers agents.

That King, Mayman and King venture survived the difficult post war years, the General Strike and the Great Depression of the 1930s

That the firm continued through those difficulties was certainly good news for the young FS who left Moseley Grammar School in 1937 at the age of 16.

Not being an academic and not really knowing what he wanted to do, FS joined his father's firm in 1938. His father's intention was to train FS as a structural engineer, but slide rules and log tables in those pre-electronic calculator days proved too much for him, and despairing of a career in structural engineering he was sent to train at Cape Asbestos Company in Barking, for whom King, Mayman and King were agents.

The outbreak of the second world war in 1939 inevitably led to a change of career direction. FS volunteered for the Army in 1940.

Top: Loading up for distribution.
Left: FGF (Aston) Ltd's premises in Princip Street.

Happily FS survived the war years unscathed and returned to Birmingham and King, Mayman and King, though not long afterwards his father died so FS began to consider expanding the firm to include other agencies.

In the early 1950s Cape Asbestos which was one of the King, Mayman and King's agencies decided to set up its own branch office at the same time offering FS a job as branch manager, but instead of accepting FS decided to branch out on his own. With a colleague for support and a single office secretary FS together with his wife Mrs DB Mayman founded Factory and Garage Furnishers Ltd, a mill furnishers, based in old shop premises in Birmingham's Prospect Row.

The business was founded in March 1954 - around that time major manufacturers of basic products were planning new plant in development areas in Scotland and South Wales.

Also for economic reasons users of such products were minimising their stocks, and demanding custom made sets to schedule, ready for immediate erection or assembly.

In a number of trades specialists stockists had been established who provided not only stock but also a manufacturing service to customers. FS Mayman saw the need for his fledgling company to act in exactly that way - as a vital link between manufacturers who wanted to maintain high output of standard products and customers who demanded ready to use materials.

In fact the progression took more than a decade to fully evolve. From starting off by distributing standardised mass-produced factory made products, that trend has been turned around in recent years. In 1974 almost two thirds of FGF's business was in distribution and little more than one third in conversion - a ratio which the organisation persists in reversing.

FGF continued to expand its operations with its establishment of sister companies to widen its markets and whereas in 1954 there had been just three staff, by 1975 the organisation comprised five companies, with 75 employees.

FGF (Continental) Ltd had been established in 1962 to tap the potential trade of what was then still the Common Market, some 11 years before Britain would

Top and above: Stages of production inside FGF.
Left: Part of FGF's fleet in the early 1990s.

despite external perceptions that this sector is in terminal decline, FGF still receives a significant number of orders for such products.

Diversification is however the key to the survival of most businesses, and FGF has been no exception to that rule. The company currently specialises in supplying and converting insulation, fire protection, ventilation and other products for the building and engineering industries.

Yet anther key to progress in Birmingham was FGF's decision to set up a dedicated processing unit for board and insulation products. That panel products division based in Bagot Street now provides internal and external architectural panels of all kinds which are distributed throughout the country.

Today the annual turnover of FGF is more than £35 million. The one time wonder material, asbestos, is of course, now history, long since replaced by safer alternatives such as glass and ceramic materials. Some 220 employees work for the company with depots in Leeds, Manchester, Bristol, Peterborough, Chatham and Southampton.

finally join the European Community. By 1975 the company was exporting a quarter of a million pounds worth of goods annually.

To what had now become FGF (Aston) Ltd was first added FGF (Northern) Ltd in 1965. The reason for this was that industry in the north was the company's largest source of customers being more highly dependant upon steam plant with the consequence needing more asbestos and 'refractories'.

FGF (Southern) Ltd was formed in 1969 to cover the southern half of England and South Wales.

In 1973 a jointly owned company Bau-Teko GmbH was established with a German company working in a similar product area to develop technical sales in Germany and German products in Britain.

For more than half a century FGF the former Factory and Garage Furnishers company, has been supplying and distributing products to construction and engineering clients across the whole of Britain and world wide export markets. Throughout all that time FS Mayman has been firmly at the helm, although now two grandsons have senior positions within the organisation, so keeping family tradition and ensuring that the FGF Group will always remain red hot.

*Above: An aerial view of FGF's Shadwell Street premises, circa 1980. **Below:** FGF's Shadwell House Headoffice, 2004.*

For the first two decades or more of its existence almost all FGF's work was for heavy industry and engineering companies. FGF supplied many of the Black Country's metal-bashers with high temperature refractive insulation for their furnaces. And,

Up for promotion

The firm of A J Gilbert (Birmingham) Ltd has been based in Buckingham Street, Hockley, for nine decades now and although the products emerging from the factory have become undeniably more sophisticated over the years the company remains true to its engineering roots.

When the original factory was opened in 1915 by Mr A J Gilbert, it was equipped simply with hand presses. These were used to manufacture metal labels from brass, steel and tin. The business continued along those lines for a number of years, first under the ownership of its founder, who converted it to a limited company in 1920, and subsequently by two brothers, Horace and Herbert Burns, who bought the business from AJ Gilbert.

During the second world war Gilbert's was taken over to fulfil Ministry of Defence orders. In the years since then however the company developed beyond simple labels and small pressings into its niche market - promotional giftware.

As Birmingham's rebuilding programme got underway Gilbert's was able to acquire the site adjoining its existing factory. This made it possible for re-building work to be carried out and a move into new premises. In 1990 the firm also acquired the building next to this site, providing a total of 32,000 square feet.

The firm employs modern production techniques to create a novel and attractive range of promotional gifts. The factory still uses hand presses, but today these are used in conjunction with other machinery such as friction screw presses, hi-tonne and hydraulic presses, HME knuckle presses, power presses, annealing ovens, rimmers, polishing lathes, sewing machines and resin applicators. There is also a fully-equipped tool room and die-sinking department. In 1996 AJ Gilbert merged with its sister

*Top: The original company premises in Buckingham Street. **Below:** Herbert Burns and his Accountant in 1952. **Right:** The workshop in the 1950s.*

however has been the Nautical Heritage side of the business: that began when the company was offered an opportunity to make memorabilia from part of the propeller from the Queen Mary, and from the main foremast of the Cutty Sark.

An AJ Gilbert subsidiary arose out of the manufacture of key-rings. Executive Key Recovery Limited is a company which specialises in recovering lost keys. Each key ring has a serial number and a return address on the back: if it is lost the key ring and any keys on it are returned to the company which is able to locate the owner of the key ring from it records.

company Executive Promotions Limited, extending the company's marketing capabilities and opening up facilities to develop customers' own designs.

Since then the company portfolio has expanded to include items as diverse as the humble fencing label or galvanising tag, through key rings, label pins, etc and machine and computer labels, to high quality gold cufflinks and sterling silver medals etc. Items can be plated in almost any available finish. Recently the company has invested heavily in machinery to give them the ability to produce coinage and medals to mint quality.

Skilled, experienced staff - combined with all the advantages of in-house manufacture - mean that customers receive much better value than they would elsewhere. Production facilities are geared towards offering total flexibility - despite millions of pieces being produced each year. All types of metals are used, but items made from leather and other materials can also be supplied. The company's own range of goods is complemented by a small selection of imported products to provide customers with a complete, across-the-range choice.

Down the years the firm has been involved in a variety of highly original and eye catching promotions. Since 2000 Gilbert's has been heavily involved in the production of commemorative coin sets both for the UK and European markets. One of the particularly innovative diversifications

With a client base spanning a wide spectrum of commerce and industry - breweries, finance houses, garages and giant corporations - design team members have plenty of scope to exercise their strong creative talents on an extremely diverse range of products. The success of the company is a tribute to its forward-looking attitude. By seizing its opportunity to expand and diversify from its old traditional product range into today's promotional gift industry, AJ Gilbert's has secured a place for British-made goods at the forefront of this competitive industry.

Today AJ Gilbert (B'Ham) Ltd is still in the hands of the Burns family, having passed from Horace and Herbert to Horace's son Tony Burns. Tony has now been joined in the business by his own son Nathan; now they, together with their co-director Lucy Cooper, are taking this unforgettable company on towards its centenary celebrations.

*Top left: A promotions stand in 1997. **Below:** A montage of staff and the AJ Gilbert premises, 2004.*

Travel news

The connection between newsagents and travel agents is not all that obvious. Some clever clogs will however surely recall that the word 'news' is derived not from a reference to reporting new events but from the initial letters of the points of the compass North, East, West and South. Newspapers got that name because of their once common practice of featuring a compass on their front pages, indicating that they published information from all parts of the globe.

One of our area's most interesting travel agencies is Darlington Travel Services based at 311 Soho Road, Handsworth. And not only is it familiar with far flung parts of the world, the business also had a long connection with newspapers.

For many years the shop was simply a newsagents and tobacconists, with a small desk upstairs where one person worked as a travel agent. Today the company is a large and busy travel agency specialising in travel to Jamaica and the Caribbean.

Despite its obvious associations with travel the company name has nothing to do with the well known northern railway town of Darlington, terminus of the world's first ever passenger railway. The business, first registered as a company in January 1944, was in fact founded by Samuel Darlington, who named the company and its original base Samuel House at 305 Soho Road, after himself.

Samuel Darlington had earlier travelled to the USA to seek his fortune, but he had returned to the United Kingdom in poor health to open a newsagents and tobacconists business in Birmingham,

Above: *An Inland Revenue document dated 1892 granting licence for Samuel Darlington to sell stamps.*
Below: *Darlingtons in the 1950s .*

the business. It would be Gary who would mastermind the change from being a newsagents and tobacconists with travel agency as merely a sideline into a fully fledged travel agents.

The company's main client base has been the large West Indian community living in and around the Midlands; as a result the business has specialised in Caribbean travel since the 1950s.

At the outset the majority of sales were for tickets for passenger ships to the West Indies when the first wave of immigrants started to revisit their homelands before returning to the United Kingdom.

a business which would later also incorporate a small travel section. Samuel Darlington believed in diversification; just selling newspapers and tobacco would never be enough for him, and older readers who knew shop in the post war years may recall that printing and stationery were early sidelines which were added to the business.

The company expanded in the 1950s acquiring other news and tobacco outlets in Birmingham, Aston, West Bromwich and Handsworth Wood. Eventually the firm would employ over 30 staff.

On Samuel Darlington's death his son Edward Darlington assumed control of the company until his retirement in the early 1960s. Edward's son Alan Darlington now took over the business, working alongside his brother-in-law, general manager and director Dennis Williams.

Following Alan Darlington's untimely death in 1971 at the age of just 39 Edward temporarily resumed the helm until the businesses were sold.

Since the 1970s, following the disposal of the retail outlets in Aston, Handsworth Wood and West Bromwich, the single office at Soho Road has focused entirely on international and domestic travel and international shipping.

What had been the Soho Road branch of the business ended up being bought by Gary Williams. Gary had started working in the newsagents shop at the age of 17, at times getting up as early as 4 am to sort out the morning papers.

By the age of 23 Gary had done all the jobs in the shop, especially on the travel side; with the owner wanting to sell up, Gary, with only five years experience under his belt, took over

With air travel becoming more accessible in the 1960s and 70s the sale of air tickets rather than transatlantic sea voyages became the company's main product.

After a few years of Gary Williams acquiring the business it had grown so much that larger premises had to be acquired and the firm moved to larger premises a few doors along Soho Road.

Today the company, now employing ten staff, is still run by Gary Williams, together with his son Robin; they pride themselves on understanding the needs and requirements of their clients, and of their unique knowledge of travel to the Caribbean.

Above: Edward Darligton (son of the founder) can be seen top left on this early organised coach trip to Palace Hotel. *Below:* Today's owner Gary Williams (standing) and son Robin .

Learning excellence

Today's Birmingham College of Food, Tourism and Creative Studies started life in the late 19th century as the Municipal Technical School. The school offered courses in cookery and domestic science.

The Technical School grew and developed under a number of different names whilst one by one new departments were added and separate buildings came into use - most recently in 2001 when an additional building was opened in Newhall Street.

It was 1968 when the Duke of Edinburgh officially opened the current premises in Summer Row. In the late 1980s came further changes and the College emerged with the name it bears today, and with a far broader range of courses. Eventually, in 1993, responsibility of the College passed from Birmingham City Council to the College's own Corporation.

With its newly established independence came various opportunities including new courses and the freedom to offer places to a greater number of students. Since 1995 the College has been an Accredited College of the University of Birmingham and all degrees and postgraduate qualifications are awarded by that institution.

The level of student achievement at the College is exceptionally high, and in 1996 the College achieved the best grades awarded

Top left: *The 1960s building site from which emerged the most successful institution in the Further Education Sector.* ***Below:*** *Lecturer Mr Klien and students pictured in the early days when the college was known as Birmingham College of Food and Domestic Arts.*

International Executive Chefs Club and the European Commission.

A third Charter Mark was awarded in 2002, whilst later that same year the College was also awarded its third 'Hospitality Assured' kitemark, an award coinciding with the transition to being a College of Higher Education.

In April 2003 the College was awarded Investors in People status for the third time whilst in June that year 'Centre of Vocational Excellence' status was achieved for the hair, beauty and holistic therapy provision of the College. What sets the College of Food, Tourism and Creative Studies apart is its involvement with the cultural and commercial life of the city, offering students direct experience in dealing with the public - experience which they find invaluable when moving into careers. In addition, European and wider international links have been established enabling students to travel and gain work experience in other parts of the world, with postgraduate programmes available in Hong Kong, the Maldives, Jamaica and Mauritius.

The needs of students, the programme content and the opportunities for career development and further study are of paramount importance, duly recognised most recently with the award of Grade 1 (Outstanding) status following a Government OFSTED inspection. The Principal and staff continue to uphold that status and carry the College forward into the future.

in a national inspection carried out by the Further Education Funding Council.

The courses offered by the College include a remarkable range of subjects: hospitality, tourism, catering, hairdressing and beauty therapy, early years care and education, bakery, leisure and sports, restaurant service, food and consumer, retail, marketing and culinary arts. The College's salons and spa operate on a commercial basis offering a range of beauty therapy treatments and hair styling.

The College boasts four training restaurants - three of which are open to the public. The Brasserie and Atrium restaurants have recently been totally refurbished. They are considered by many to be amongst the best places to eat in the Midlands. There is something for everyone, whether the customer wants to dine out in style or simply enjoy a quick pub snack in the College's Cap and Gown restaurant.

The Brasserie has been at the forefront in providing experience and scope for the talents of students preparing to take up hotel and restaurant management. They organise regular theme nights at the Brasserie from the 'swingin 60s' to the 'gun totin' Wild West. Live music and a menu designed in keeping with the theme each play their part in making theme nights fun for all.

Student accommodation is now at The Maltings, off Broad Street, offering over 800 en-suite study bedrooms, a large sports hall, fitness suite, shop and bar.

Students on the adventure tourism and sports and leisure courses use the facilities at Edgbaston Reservoir as part of their training.

In 2001 the College was named as a Pathfinder Centre of Vocational Excellence for Catering and Hospitality.

Also in 2001, and again in 2003, the College was proclaimed the Best Hotel School in the UK by the

Top left: Princess Anne visits the award-winning college in 2000. *Below:* The impressive College entrance, 2004.

Welding Sparkes

There's an old riddle engineers used to ask their children 'What do you get if you feed a cat with calcium carbide? The answer: 'A set o' lean kittens'. Mystified ? It's wordplay on 'acetylene' the highly combustible gas given off when water is added to powdered calcium carbide. It's been along time since anyone asked that particular riddle though we bet it was one heard often enough back in the days when one of our city's best known industrial supplies companies was founded.

Birmingham's Midland Welding Supply Company began its life in 1921 as a calcium carbide supplier to the Midland's motor industry. The motor industry needed the product for generating the acetylene gas used for welding and brazing.

Founded by two cousins Eric and Harold Edge working on their own, the company acquired its present name in 1922.

Top: *An early Edge & Co. letterhead.*
Below: *Harry Sparkes.*

In 1927 British Oxygen Company (B.O.C) introduced Dissolved Acetylene 'DA' in bottles to the Motor Industry. Overnight sales of Calcium Carbide plummeted. The company responded by extending its business, significantly widening the range of welding consumables and associated products it supplied.

In 1928 the Edge cousins took on a 15 year old office boy, Harry Sparkes who would eventually have an immense impact on the business.

Originally Midland Welding was located in the Birmingham Bull Ring, but as a result of the second world war the company relocated to new premises at Hall Green.

During the war Harry was reserved from the forces and spent part of those years training welders; the rest of the time he spent welding parts for Sten guns in a little engineering shop in Showell Green Lane. And in his spare time Harry was a member of the fire service!

In the immediate post war years Harry Sparkes would go to Leicester on the train taking his bike with him. Staying at a Bed and breakfast above a fish and chip shop he would cycle around Leicester searching out orders which were then despatched by parcel post, road carrier and train. In 1954 one of the Edge cousins was killed in a road traffic accident and Harry was made Managing Director. The second Edge cousin died in the mid 1960s. The Edge family involvement in the business would come to an end in 1980 when the last of the Edge cousins' widows died.

In 1974 additional premises were bought in the Reddicap Trading Estate at Sutton Coldfield for extended warehousing, and as a secure location for the company's fleet of vehicles. Another company was acquired in 1994, East Midland Welding in Nottingham, which provided a broader platform for services and deliveries to the East Midlands.

In 1996, the year of Harry Sparkes' death, the Birmingham branches relocated to new purpose built premises alongside the National Exhibition Centre and the Birmingham International Airport giving the company easy access to all motorway links and increasing its capacity for storage and the opportunity for commercial expansion.

Today Midland Welding is one of the country's largest distributors of its kind, priding itself on the fact that it is

Top: Loading up in the 1970s. **Right:** *Managing Director of Midland Welding Supply Company since 1984 Derek Sparkes and wife Bronwyn.*

master distributor of most major branded welding consumables and plant. This allows the company to give its customers the product flexibility and choice needed in modern manufacturing. The company is the largest welding distributor in the Midlands and supplies most of the major motor manufacturers.

The company specialises in the prompt supply of plant and consumables to its customers, delivering twice daily within the Birmingham area, along with servicing and calibrating all welding machines. The company has its own gas inspection engineers, service engineers and technical representatives who can offer advice and help on site at very short notice.

In the 21st century Midland Welding remains a family business despite having grown considerably from its original two cousins and an office boy; its growth and reputation were

created by the late Harry Sparkes and by his son Derek, who joined the firm in 1971 and who has been the Managing Director since 1984. Derek Sparkes continues to adopt the tradition of a personal approach pioneered by his father, ensuring a continuation of the high standards of service through which the company has achieved its enviable position.

On the right line

How our roads and urban environment have changed over the course of the last sixty years or so. Until the 1950s most of our back streets were still cobbled: indeed many of our so-called main roads only had a strip of tarmac down the middle. And what about all those white lines and yellow lines?

White lines of course were a fairly early arrival, but who, in say 1960, would ever have dreamed that by the end of the century hardly a yard of our roads would be without some indication of the line marker's activities?

Top: The terrace of the Botanical Gardens in Edgebaston which was surfaced by Grosvenor Workman, 1935. Below: Durolas begin work for the surfacing of Summerfield Park in March 1951. Right: An early contract for Durolas was to lay the Asphalt at the Guy factory in Wolverhampton.

Help crossing the road? We didn't even have zebra crossings. Once upon a time we thought Belisha beacons, named after the then Minister of Transport, were the bees knees: we'd never had thought up pelican crossings and flashing green men in our wildest dreams.

One item of street furniture we were already long familiar with however were cats eyes, reflecting road studs to give them their proper name, and invented in the 1920s by Halifax man Percy Shaw. In the days when street lights were fewer and further between cats eyes were a real blessing for the motorist driving at night, and a magnet for small boys with penknives anxious to discover how they worked.

But who has been doing all this work down the passing years? Who is it that has so transformed our roads over the course of a few generations? 'The Government' some will

Originally the company constructed and resurfaced drives and car parks, carrying out work at many country estates in the Midlands. Additional departments were later formed for road marking and fencing. In 1950 Durolas laid the first zebra crossing in Birmingham for the City Corporation.

In October 1996 Durolas laid the natural stone paving around the Hall of Memory; the company also carried out most of the fencing work around Birmingham Airport.

Today the firm has become one of the Midlands best known and well respected local businesses. It employs over 50 people and has an annual turnover of some £4 million, carrying out work for Local Authorities, hospitals, schools and many private clients.

respond, citing the various Road Traffic Acts passed by Parliament. A more practical answer however is the companies which won contracts to be commissioned to carry out such works. And in Birmingham the best known of those firms is Durolas.

Now based at 95 Frances Road, Kings Norton, Durolas (Contractors) Ltd began life as a separate company only in 1947 after having previously operated as a department of Grosvenor Workman, based then at 280 Broad Street.

Grosvenor Workman was then a supplier of high class gardening equipment and sundries but owned several other businesses in the area: the proprietor was the eponymous Mr Grosvenor Workman himself. The firm carried out surfacing works at the Botanical Gardens, Edgbaston in September 1935; the same area was resurfaced by Durolas in time for former US President Bill Clinton's visit in May 1998.

Just after the second world war, following the untimely death of Mr Grosvenor Workman, Durolas (Contractors) Limited was formed, with Mrs EE Grosvenor Workman as Chairman, and Richard (Dick) Morris as Managing Director.

Durolas' original offices were just around the corner from Broad Street, at numbers 7-15 Gas Street, where ITV is now to be found. The company also had yards in Grosvenor Street West and Anderton Street.

Over the decades Dick Morris would be succeeded as Managing Director by Vernon Morgan and Eddie Brookes, and by today's MD, John Dark.

The company still has members of the Workman family as its major share holders. Mrs Grosvenor Workman died only in 1998, at the grand age of 102. David Workman, grandson of the founder, is the current Chairman.

In 2003 the company was the winner of the Considerate Contractors Gold award from Birmingham City Council.

As for the future, the effectiveness of being a successful Surfacing Contractor, combining Road Marking and Fencing, Durolas will surely still be working flat out in the 22nd century!

*Top: Durolas laying the first Zebra Crossing for the Corporation in 1950. **Above left:** Road lining.*
Below: *In 2003 Durolas received the winners of the Considerate Contractors Award from Birmingham City Council.*

Luck and brass

As he collected spilled coal at a South Wales colliery it could never have entered 14 year old Harold McGrail's mind that one day he might be lucky enough to be the head of a prestigious Birmingham brass foundry.

Harold McGrail first came to the Midlands to work at Aston brassfounders Barkers. From there he moved to Ashby's in Buckingham Street, which produced cabinet hardware.

Ashby's however suffered severe financial problems which led to the firm moving to Pullen's brass foundry in Moland Street, where Harold became its manager.

The owner died in 1931, and in partnership with Thomas Armstrong and the help of a major customer, Mr G Warshaw, Harold took over. The two partners combined their names to call their business Armac - the name which endures to this day.

The partnership was short-lived, and within a year Harold, with his younger brother Tom and his sister Eileen, was the owner of the Armac brass foundry making cabinet hardware.

It was of course a terrible time to set out in business; sometimes staff could not be paid until customers had paid their debts.

The war would prove the firm's saviour. Despite losing many employees to both the services and the Spitfire assembly plant at Castle Bromwich Armac managed to be registered for war work. It produced portholes for ships and components for radar equipment.

In the 1950s brass was rationed, but as the British economy began to recover from the effects of the war so the company too began to prosper.

Top: Founder, Harold McGrail.
Right: *A view inside the workshop in the 1970s.* ***Above right:*** *Armac's 1970s premises.*

In 1958 a move was made from the original premises to better accommodation around the corner in Staniforth Street.

The company suffered a serious set back in 1980 when a fire led to major disruption. As a result the factory had to be rebuilt. At the same time an economic recession hit Britain. Having beaten these twin disasters the firm had to face a second, even worse, recession in the 1990s.

But through thick and thin the family tradition had been maintained: firstly in 1960 when Harold's son Bryan joined the firm; he assumed control in 1980 when Harold retired. Bryan would in turn become Chairman and his three sons take control, of what had become the Armac group of five local companies, each involved in differing aspects of the brass foundry business.

In the early days the work had been very labour intensive, with belt-driven polishing and turning lathes working exclusively in brass sand-castings.

By the 1990s the Staniforth Street premises were very different from what they had been in 1958. The modern plant was equipped with large CNC machines and automatic finishing equipment, working in a multitude of brass components from several sources.

Emphasis had switched to hot brass forgings, pressure die-castings, turned parts, pressed work as well as the traditional sand castings.

Bryan McGrail died in March 2004. He had been instrumental in driving the company into the modern age and steering it through two major recessions. He had expanded the Group with the purchase of Bentley Brassworks in Walsall and begun negotiations to purchase Armac's main customer, Martin & Co.

In 2003 Armac was approached by property developers wanting to bulldoze the Armac site to build student accommodation for Aston University.

The deal enabled Armac to move to new premises in Duddeston two miles away, and to conclude the purchase of Martin & Co.

The new Chairman Nicholas McGail, and his brothers Paul and Mark, have since merged Armac with Bentley Brassworks and with the engineering company Brass Turned Parts to create one large business. Manufacturing is under one roof, and with Martin & Co also accommodated the first steps into the distribution side of the business have now been taken.

The company's main markets remain in the reproduction furniture industry and antique restoration trade.

Armac's reputation for high quality, especially in its meticulous finishing techniques, the authenticity of design and the wide range of products has made its name known throughout Britain and abroad. Despite the company having to continuously compete against inferior imports, and cheaper alternatives, furniture makers the world over recognise and appreciate the quality of Armac's products; they know exactly how lucky we are that young Harold McGrail left Wales for Birmingham.

Top left: An aerial view of Armac's Staniforth Street premises before being re-developed into accommodation for students of Aston University.
Left: Bryan McGrail, Chairmain up until 2004. Below: Armac's new Duddeston premises, 2004.

The best years of their lives

The second half of the 19th century was a period of radical change in attitudes to education. Many new schools were opened; the majority of independent ones however were for boys only.

In December 1875 Edgbaston manufacturer George Dixon sent a circular to 52 leading local families inviting them to join him to discuss the 'propriety of establishing a High School for Girls in Edgbaston'.

At the subsequent meeting it was proposed to set up a modern, independent, non-sectarian girls' day school. Distinguished local families from both Quaker and Unitarian backgrounds, including the Allbrights, Beales, Crosskeys, Chamberlains, Dales, Dawsons, Frys, Kenricks, Lloyds, Martineaus, Sturges and Wilsons agreed with the proposal and joined together to support the founding of Edgbaston High School.

The school's first premises were at 284 Hagley Road (subsequently the site of the Marriott Swallow Hotel). Miss Alice Jane Cooper was appointed the school's first headmistress, a position she was to hold for 20 years.

The school opened in 1876, following entrance examinations at which 76 girls were successful. Very soon however, it became necessary to extend the building; within two years the school roll had doubled in size, and to accommodate it The Laurels at 280 Hagley Road was acquired.

Under Miss Cooper the school was quick to attain high academic standards. By 1881 one girl had already won a scholarship to Oxford, and before long many others would go on to obtain Oxbridge degrees.

Miss Cooper was also a keen advocate of extra-curricular activities; various clubs and societies were set up, though the girls' enthusiastic participation in cricket matches must have raised several eyebrows.

A school magazine was launched entitled 'Laurel Leaves' which recounted the life of the school in those now long gone late Victorian days.

Top: Miss Cooper and her staff.
Left: A hockey team in the 1890s.
Below: The front of the school in 1951.

founders, seeking to foster a wide breadth of educational opportunity based on the academic curriculum at the heart of the school, and to ensure that all its pupils benefit from this.

EHS is one of the country's leading independent schools, and is the only school of its size in Birmingham to offer a complete continuity of primary and secondary girls-only education. It is a lively, caring school which reflects the multi-cultural life of Birmingham, and one in which a strong sense of community and involvement is paramount. The girls receive a stimulating and challenging education. Former pupils of Edgbaston High School will happily testify to the school's success in building confidence in its girls, developing their abilities and sending out lively young women who are fully equipped to make a valuable all round contribution to society.

Following Miss Cooper's retirement in 1895 Miss Eliza Japp became headmistress; she introduced hockey, medical inspections, uniforms and the boarding house before resigning in 1899 to marry and return to her native Scotland.

Miss Tarleton Young now became headmistress; she was responsible for the addition of the gymnasium and the Preparatory School before leaving in 1924 after a quarter of a century at the helm.

Subsequent headmistresses have included Miss Winifred Casswell who guided the school through the difficult years of the second world war, and Miss Edith Hopkins whose boundless energy proved invaluable when in 1963 the school, now numbering some 860 pupils, moved to its current site on Westbourne Road.

Today this 14 acre site offers excellent facilities which are constantly being refurbished and updated under a rolling programme. The Pre-Preparatory, the Preparatory Department and the Senior School each have their own separate purpose-built accommodation. There are three hockey pitches, an athletics track, 12 all-weather tennis courts and a heated indoor swimming pool. An art block was built in 1985 and a new Music School added in 1992 as well as a new wing with a large IT Centre, new laboratories and an updated and enlarged Home Economics Department opened in 1994.

The Octagon, a new £3.5 million building opened in 2004, incorporating a new Nursery, in addition to an arena with retractable seating for 660 which will inevitably enhance the school's reputation for dance and drama.

Today Edgbaston High School with its excellent modern facilities continues to build on the traditions of its

The school's current Headmistress is Elizabeth Mullenger.

Top: The Laurels gym in 1957. *Left: Elizabeth Mullenger, Headmistress of Edgbaston High School for Girls since 1998.* ***Below:*** *The new £3.5 million Octagon opened in 2004.*

Cookings' essential ingredient

Samuel Groves & Co. Limited were established in 1817 in Hockley, Birmingham and were engaged in the manufacture of Cooking Utensils, Household Trays and Metal Pressings which were sold to other manufacturers for use in their products.

One of the mainstays of the Company, were products manufactured for home and industry including catering and household trays, ash trays, letter racks and crumb scoops. These were very ornate in design and manufactured in a variety of metals and finishes. The trade name for one such range of these products was 'Carpathian' and the products were available in nickel plated silver, copper and brass. There were 130 different sizes of trays and all were of a hand polished finish with an average selling price in 1921 of £0/18/4d per dozen which today equates to .91p per dozen or .07p each - in their day these were not cheap items, indeed they were the thing to purchase and look after.

'Brummie Metal Bashers' they may have been, but in the early 1920s the company perfected a process for producing machine-engraved designs on metal plates of all descriptions. The designs were not embossed but were cut into the thickness of the metal, leaving a clear flat surface at the back. This was especially good for producing Branded goods and novelties, which the company was famous for.

In fact the company still produces Branded Trays and other items and has recently manufactured products for Martell, Schweppes, St Moritz and Red Bull.

This tradition of manufacturing carries on to the present day and indeed some of the many products produced, including Metal Trays and Ashtrays on sale from 1817, were still listed in the company's Catalogue in 1921 and are still being sold today. It would appear that the crocodile skin design, was branded 'Sirius' which has been appreciated throughout the years, carries on to this day and probably will for some time to come.

In addition to these products the company also manufactured Hand-Hammered Art Pewter Ware, which was branded 'Roundhead.' Innovators in their day, Samuel Groves's engineers used a leadless pewter of a special composition which combined a beautiful silver white appearance with great strength and durability. The products were white throughout, were non tarnishing and the company said they were "The Heirlooms of Posterity". Indeed they were - and they were also sold around the world. In the mid 1920s their Art Deco Pewter products sold all over the world and today the designs look as if they are straight off the drawing board. An interesting note is that it was necessary to issue a caution to customers against purchasing imitations - so nothing in business has really changed only yesterday it was pewter.

As the years progressed the company's sound reputation for the quality of its manufacturing expertise became apparent and quite apart from trays and pewter products, the government, in the form of the War

Top: *Groves factory in Musgrove Road, Hoeckley.*
Above: *Examples of trays produces by Samuel Groves.*

Office, also called on the company to produce products - one product in particular the ammunition box - was in it's day and probably still is, the most dreaded piece of equipment for the Army to train with or carry around battlefields. Even when empty they still seems to weigh a ton or is it tonne? Indeed some of the pictures in this article were stored in one such box, which has a stamped brass plate, S. Groves, B'ham and is dated 1916. Perhaps a quality reject then, but today a Company heirloom.

Moving onward to more recent times the company moved from its 1900 base in Musgrave Road to a modern factory at Norton Street, Hockley in the 1950s, where it now employs 140 people and at one time was visited by the late HM the Queen, the Queen Mother. The Company, which is British Standard EN ISO 9001 qualified, now produces bakeware, cookware and utensils from materials as diverse as aluminium, mild steel, copper and stainless steel. These products, in all about 1200 items, are manufactured with the trade names "Longlife" "Le Buffet" and "Connoisseur" are sold into the catering industry. "Longlife" aluminium cookware has been manufactured since the raw material became available in 1912. At that time the aluminium cost would have been higher in pounds sterling than it is almost today. The company then embarked on manufacturing kettles, colanders, straight and bellied pans and all other items of cookware for which it has been famous for, ever since. An interesting note is that Samuel Groves & Co. produce a casserole pot which would keep a family of four fed with 1/2 pint of soup per person per day - for a month without running out!

Longlife Utensils

The 'Longlife' name remains one of the best-respected trade marks in the catering industry today and anyone eating out will definitely have been served food with or served themselves with 'Le Buffet' or ' Connoisseur' utensils.

For the retail market the company uses the trade name "Mermaid". In the range are standard catering bakeware items manufactured from aluminium and given an extra innovative process called 'Hard Anodising'. Hard anodised as opposed to anodised or soft anodised is a finishing process, which is second only in hardness to diamonds. Indeed, T.V's most popular and respected Chef, Delia Smith, said that the Samuel Groves "Mermaid" hard anodised range of bakeware was the best on the market. Sales of these products rose considerably along with the "Little Gem" Cookware products she also commended. They are also used by all current T.V. Chefs - they really are the best bakeware products on the market today. If you are a serious cook, even if you do not know Samuel Groves make them in Birmingham, then you will certainly know the name

Today, Samuel Groves & Co. Limited, the largest manufacturer of catering utensils in the UK are owned by the Birmingham based Metalrax Group plc.

Roger Brain the Chief Executive with Shirley Dodd, Director and Richard Barrett in charge of Sales and Marketing, are entrusted with pushing the company forward into the 21st century. Today as so many years ago, innovation, an experienced workforce, using state of the art machinery, competing and selling throughout the world keeps Samuel Groves in the forefront of technology even if some of the products really do have a good black hard anodised finish, the company has a polished stainless steel bright future. As Samuel Groves say - we really are 'Cooking's Essential Ingredient.'

Top: Roundhead Hand-Hammered Art Pewter Ware.
Below: Part of Caterers Cookware.

Pressed for choice

Birmingham's brass industry had its origins in the 1740s. A century later one of the city's best known manufacturers of brass parts was founded, S Lilley & Son Ltd.

The business was started around 1840 by Simeon Lilley, a master metal stamper and piercer. Simeon was one of ten children born to William and Harriet Lilley; he himself would have four sons, two of whom, Walter and Alfred, would eventually work in the business.

Some of the firm's earliest products were detonator explosives for the railways and cylinder fog signals. Door and cupboard furniture including drop handles, studs and latch locks followed. Other memorable products included The Imperial'

Above: Founder, Simeon Lilley.
Below: S. Lilley & Son's 80 Alcester Street premises.
Right: Capstan Shop, 1920s.

crystal wireless set first produced in 1918, and the 'Golden' series of terminals and plugs for the radio trade as well as electrical lamp holders.

A seemingly endless stream of products has flowed from the factory: shutter knobs, kettle knobs, can knobs, cupboard turns, sash fasteners, cups and screws, cycle stampings, pedal caps, adjustment tips, tape buckles, clips, ferrules and washers; small stampings for the electrical trade; brass lamp holders to conduit bushes. Today a complete wiring service is offered for

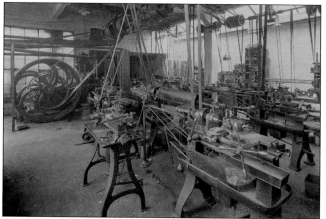

the lamp bases and fittings, and whilst a vast range of items are available from stock the company also offers a bespoke service producing pressed or turned parts to customers' own specifications.

For generations the business has remained a family firm, and today the staff still includes half a dozen members of the Lilley family.

The founder originally occupied premises at the Star Works in Bordesley Street then moved to at 8 Birchall Street before ending up at the company's present location at 75-80 Alcester Street.

Alfred Ernest Lilley became an equal partner with his father in 1893. The business was then valued at £100-150, a valuation which included plant and tools but no stock. Alfred injected another £50-60 of his own capital into the business. It was agreed that Simeon's shares would be willed to Alfred on his death. As a consequence Alfred became sole owner of the business on 26th October 1902.

The Great War of 1914-18 saw the company employing 100 workers to produce 'friction tube strikers' along with lamp holders for the Army and the Admiralty.

Apparent long term success in any business however usually masks a series of difficulties overcome. S Lilley & Son is no exception. In 1981 for example a fire destroyed the company's warehouse. But that disaster pales to insignificance with the catastrophe which struck in the 1940s.

During the second world war S Lilley & Son's workers contributed to the war effort producing parts for Yale locks, respirator parts, sockets, ferrules and lamp holders for the armed forces.

The factory was bombed in November 1940, and most of the old building destroyed. The only part which survives is the 'capstan shop'. But that calamity was only a foretaste of the disaster yet to come.

In April 1941 a German plane dropped its bomb load as it was being chased from the skies above the city centre. The siren had given the all clear and at that moment the Lilley family were moving back into their houses from their shelter. The bombs destroyed both homes of Alfred and Phillip Lilley, which were situated in Robin Hood Lane. Alfred and Ellen Lilley were killed along with their oldest son Joseph. Phillip was fire watching with his son Lesley at the factory in Birmingham, however the bomb also claimed the lives of Phillip's wife Ellen and their daughter Phyllis.

Remarkably the surviving members of the family were able to salvage what was left of their lives and the business, laying the foundations of today's S Lilley & Son.

Often referred to as the 'Rolls Royce' end of the lighting sector today Lilley's products are now sold across the world.

Customers include DIY stores, lamp manufactures and electrical wholesalers.

And though the exceptional quality has remained unaltered there have been changes: today there are just 34 staff. Over the years there has been a steady reduction in labour as machines have become more complex. Jobs that once took nine machines can now be produced by one machine in a fraction of the time.

In 2001 Colmore Pressings Ltd merged with S Lilley & Son vastly increasing the range of pressed products this remarkable company is now able to offer.

Top: *Tool Room, 1920s.*
Above left: *An early company vehicle circa 1955.*
Below: *A montage of the S. Lilley & Son Ltd plant and modern machinery, 2001.*

When the name fits...

The years following the end of the second world war were ones full of mixed emotions. Our sense of triumph was mixed with sadness: we had won a war but lost many of our best young men. And many older heads recalled the terrible economic recession which had engulfed the world in the decades following the end of the first world war. But by contrast with their elders however many optimistic young men were convinced that the 1950s would not be a re-run of the 'hungry thirties' but instead be a decade of opportunity.

The year 1953 was dominated by the Queen Elizabeth II's coronation. The newspaper headlines also featured accounts of the first ascent of Mount Everest by the

partnership of Edmund (later Sir Edmund) Hillary and the Sherpa, Tensing Norgay.

In Birmingham, and quite unheralded, another kind of heights-scaling partnership was being created by two brothers, John and George Neil.

Little could the brothers have then guessed that more than half a century later their partnership would be a leading Architectural Ironmongery firm named Doorfit, who are also locksmiths and garage door distributors. The company are today based at Icknield House, Heaton Street, Hockley.

*Above: The company's original premises in Vyse Street, 1953. **Right and below:** Founders John Neil and George Neil (centre) pictured with the Doorfit staff outside the company premises in the late 1970s.*

After George Neil had served in the Royal Navy and his brother John in the Royal Air Force both were keen to start a business together.

With so many houses and other buildings having been destroyed during the course of the second world war the building industry seemed promising; and so the pair agreed to start a builders' ironmongery firm.

George had already spent some years in the ironmongery trade, so fortunately the two brothers did already have some contacts to help them get started.

The name Doorfit was coined whilst the pair searched around the city looking for suitable premises. They eventually located a building in Vyse Street, premises where the firm would stay for the next 27 years.

The business became incorporated as a limited company, Doorfit Products Ltd, in 1958.

During the late 1960s the company established a garage door section, and in due course would become a major distributor. Fellow director, Alan George, has headed that division for over four decades.

In 1976 the company suffered a serious fire at Vyse Street caused by an electrical fault; as a consequence John and George were prompted to consider moving. It was an opportunity to build new, larger premises.

Within a year suitable land had been found in Heaton Street, owned by the Council. A deal was negotiated with the Council for a brand new building and the company moved into its new corporate headquarters, Icknield House, over the August Bank Holiday weekend in 1979. Sadly co-founder George Neil would die less than a year later, though

he could already feel immense pride and satisfaction in what he and his brother John had achieved in the 27 years since they had started out on their joint venture.

By then, from its original workforce of just two in 1953, staff number had by now risen to 35.

Eight years on from George Neil's death, under pressure to expand again, a new showroom and warehouse were built for the company's Garage Door division, which was occupied in 1988.

Subsequently a Locksmith section would be established, a section greatly enhanced by the acquisition of another firm, JHS Security, enabling the company to now offer full master-key suites from its own in-house facilities.

Today the company offers its clients, Architects, Builders, industry and the general public a fine service as a modern version of the old fashioned ironmonger in addition to offering its garage doors and spares as well as its locksmiths service. Staff number have grown along with the business, and have now reached 70.

Having been founded by two brothers Doorfit is today benefiting from a similar pairing. John Neil's sons, Philip and Robert are now both part of the business. Philip Neil is Operations Director and Robert Neil is Sales Director.

Having celebrated its Golden Jubilee in 2003 Birmingham's Doorfit is now looking forward to many more decades in business, and to planting the firm's flag on even higher peaks.

Top: *Doorfit staff pictured in 1991.*
Left: *The Neil family 2004, John (centre) and sons Philip (left) and Robert (right).*

Learning for life

Founded by George Cadbury in 1909, Fircroft College of Adult Education is an educational charity providing higher and general education opportunities in a residential environment.

Initially only for men, since 1980 the College has also included women on all its courses. The College is situated in a large, early 20th century, family residence 'Primrose Hill', George Cadbury's own former home, set in 6 acres of gardens and grounds in Bristol Road, Selly Oak.

The college however began its life based at The Dell, in Oak Tree Lane. For its first five years Fircroft flourished. Correspondence courses were started and even summer schools for women were held in 1910.

George Cadbury's vision was to provide an education which was generally broadening, not simply the means by which men might become qualified to do better jobs; he envisaged mature men aged 25 to 35 coming to study groups of subjects such as economics, history, art and drama. But whatever the subject they would gain something more important, namely the art of living together in a group of 40 to 50 students which he believed developed the character and enlarged the mind.

During the first world war The Dell was taken over as a hospital and the remaining staff transferred to Holland House, Woodbrooke.

Between the wars Fircroft again flourished. It was recognised by the Department

Top: Founder, George Cadbury.
Above right: Staff and students of 1920-1921.
Right: The original Fircroft College in Oak Tree Lane.

of Education in 1925, but still remained wholly dependent upon George Cadbury.

In 1939 war closed Fircroft for a second time and the Dell was turned into a remand home. Fircroft re-opened in Oak Tree Lane in 1947 by which time temporary buildings were already in use at Primrose Hill.

After George Cadbury's death in 1954 Fircroft had to become self supporting. Cadbury's son, Christopher, became chairman of the Trust and Governors. In 1957 Christopher Cadbury moved the college to the Cadbury family home, Primrose Hill.

Fircroft would justify George Cadbury's convictions and effort by providing thousands of young adults with the opportunity to take time off from the driving necessity of earning a living in order to consider the

In 2002/2003, of the 1,306 students, 79 per cent were female, 42 per cent from ethnic minorities, 5 per cent were disabled, 89 per cent were over the age of 25 and 56 percent were unemployed or without a source of income.

The College will soon open new facilities costing £1.5 million. The programme of work includes a new purpose built teaching block as well as increasing the en suite residential facilities.

The College's current programme remains true to George Cadbury's vision. 'Fircroft Studies' is a one year full time programme of key skills plus units in history, literature and social science. There is also the option of a community placement. This now leads to a nationally recognised Access Certificate which enables the majority of students to progress to university. There is also an expanding short courses programme aimed at personal, professional and political development. Many are designed around the needs of the voluntary and community sector, and there are specific courses for those wanting to explore future options in learning and work.

purpose of life. It enriched their minds and their person-alities; and through them Fircroft's humanitarian and liberal influences would extend into countless other lives.

Inevitably many students whose horizons were extended and whose academic talents were nurtured eventually left their previous occupations to take on more demanding work, as ministers of religion, social workers, trade union officials, politicians, lawyers and managers. One of the first students became Birmingham's first probation officer, another became Lord Mayor and others were elected Members of Parliament. Many more however returned to their jobs and helped raise the standards of their colleagues, in accordance with the aims of the founder.

The College now has a long history of enabling adult learners to have a second chance of education, many of whom have had a number of unsuccessful and alienating learning experiences during and after leaving school. Students come with a wide range of learning and support needs as well as needing to develop interpersonal and group skills. Many also come from disadvantaged social or economic backgrounds.

Top left: Fircroft College in the late 1950s.
Above left: Fircroft College 2004. ***Top right:*** *Plans for the new purpose built teaching block and residential facilities.* ***Below:*** *Staff and students pictured in the summer of 2004.*

Fair for Birmingham

In the second half of the 19th century the Birmingham Town Mission did much charitable work. The Mission's principal aim was to 'alleviate the sufferings of the poor and others in extreme distress' by providing 'shelter, board and clothing'.

During 1872 however the Town Mission set itself two new objectives: to provide a Mission for local cabmen, and religious instruction for the 'deaf and dumb'.

The former objective was achieved by the opening of the Cabmen's Rest in Ratcliffe Place, and the latter by the appointment of a 'Missioner', Mr WA Griffiths.

WA Griffiths was one of at least 80 profoundly deaf inhabitants of Birmingham; there were thought to be another 30 or so living in the Black Country. His work included giving religious services and lectures to

Right: *Members enjoying a game of cards.*
Below: *Standing room only at the Christmas Pantomime.*

groups which met in school rooms at Graham Street, and in visiting deaf people in their homes.

In 1873 subscriptions were invited specifically for the use of the 'Mission to the Deaf and Dumb' and there was much talk of raising funds to provide deaf people with a Mission Hall of their own. The Birmingham and

In subsequent years an emphasis would be placed on supporting deaf people within the community. BID's initiatives in that sphere have included creating an Employment Service to help deaf people find jobs, and a scheme launched in 1994 to train deaf people as tutors of sign language. An interpreting unit was established in 1994 and a new deaf care domiciliary service was pioneered in 1993.

In 1997 Lottery funding made it possible to launch an Information Service and Newspaper - 'Sign Times'. Since then the Information Service grown to include a video production service, producing and translating videos into BSL. A resource library has been established, containing books videos and other materials for the deaf community and those with an interest in it. A Volunteer Service now aims to get deaf people to volunteer within their own community.

The Interpreting Service has grown to meet the ever increasing demand, whilst the provision of Sign Language courses to an advanced level has been increased.

A full time Youth and Community Development worker is now employed to ensure that an investment is made in local young deaf people, this has led to young deaf people becoming UNICEF representatives and UK Youth Parliament representatives.

Looking to the future it is hoped that a new Deaf Centre will eventually become a cultural focus for deaf people across the whole Midlands.

Top: A group of members marvel at the first telecommunications device (the 'teleprinter') for deaf people. How things have moved on in the age of e-mail and mobile phones! *Below:* The Centre for Deaf People shortly after its opening in 1973.

Midland Adult Deaf and Dumb Association, founded in 1899 as the Institute for Adult Deaf and Dumb in Birmingham, took over from the Town Mission in 1906, employing Mr Griffiths as Missioner. It provided premises in which to hold meetings, first at the Police Institute in James Watt Street then in the former Bible Hall in Broad Street.

WA Griffiths retired in 1917, partly because of the growing trend towards oral teaching instead of finger spelling and signing, his own preferred means of communication.

The good work of the Institute however continued. Finally in 1932 sufficient funds had been raised to convert a warehouse and stables in Granville Street into a centre for the deaf and dumb - the Birmingham Institute for the Deaf, the word dumb having by this time been dropped. BID became the first voluntary charity in the United Kingdom to be officially responsible for providing the welfare services which the local authority was legally required to provide for the deaf community under the 1948 National Assistance Act.

Under the guidance of Eric Ashton who led the organisation for over 30 years, the Institute continued to grow, not least through the development of the Birmingham Deaf Sports and Social Club. By the early 1970s however, the Granville Street centre had become overcrowded and an appeal was launched to raise £57,000 enabling the Institute to move to its present premises in Ladywood Road.

Pioneering work continued when in 1984 BID began working with BBC Midlands Today team at Pebble Mill to produce the first news bulletins with sign language. In 1985 it established the first of two residential homes. Wye Cliff was the first locally run rehabilitation unit for deaf people in the country, set up in partnership with Midland Area Housing Association.

Never tired nor exhausted

Located next to the inner ring road in the Waterlinks area of Birmingham, the Lodge Tyre Company is familiar to many thousands of the city's motorists, as well as to its many commercial and agricultural clients. And with seven other depots around the Midlands, in Alsager, Coventry, Leicester Nottingham, Stoke-on-Trent, Telford and Walsall, it's not just Birmingham folk who recognise the Lodge Tyre name.

With its fleet of over forty breakdown vans plying the roads, this independent family company is proud to be able to still offer the same level of personal service begun by its founder in the 1930s.

The foundations of the rubber tyre industry had been laid nearly a century earlier when in 1839 the American Charles Goodyear had discovered that by heating rubber latex with sulphur it could be hardened yet still remain flexible. Goodyear's process, which he dubbed 'vulcanisation' would later be put to memorable use by Scottish inventor John Dunlop. In 1887 Charles Dunlop developed a commercial practical version of an idea first patented in 1846 by RW Thomas - the pneumatic tyre.

Within a few years pneumatic rubber tyres were to be found everywhere, and a large industry had been spawned, one which would grow ever more massive as the 20th century progressed.

The Lodge Tyre business was founded in 1936 by George Edmund Lodge. George had until then been an accountant but at the age of 26 decided to have a go at selling car tyres.

Starting a new business in the middle of the hungry thirties, the very epicentre of the world wide economic depression, may not seem like a good idea; yet it did make sense. Most industry was depressed, but surprisingly the motor industry was still creeping upwards; inexorably the number of motor cars on

the road was increasing as the economy and convenience of the petrol engine over horse and cart or public transport became increasingly apparent.

With two staff working for him George began to sell tyres from premises on the corner of Rea Street and Bradford Street.

By the 1960s the company had relocated three times; firstly in 1946 to Bloomsbury Street, followed in the 1950s with a move to Ashstead Row before settling at the current premises in Lord Street in 1963.

The journey to Lord Street was not however quite so straightforward as it might sound. George was missing for six years

between 1939 and 1945, serving as a sergeant in the Royal Engineers. His wife Catherine kept the business afloat, but inevitably it had run down considerably during the war years. As the Japanese had overrun the rubber plantations of the Far East, and most other available supplies of rubber were diverted to military use, motorists in petrol-rationed Britain had to make do and mend if they had a puncture.

A continuing post-war shortage of rubber meant that repairs became an important part of the business, with equipment for vulcanisation being essential.

In the 1960s George Lodge was followed in the business by his son Martin George Lodge, and with help from Robert Clarke they developed a successful business in the Birmingham area.

Lodge Tyre today is run by the third generation of the founder's family: Andy and Simon Christmas and Martyn Lodge, all three George Lodge's grandchildren.

In addition to its depots, offering exhausts, shock absorbers, car servicing and MOTs, Lodge Tyre also has two manufacturing plants in Birmingham producing premium quality remoulds and retreads. The plants use computer aided manufacturing systems aided by laser technology. As a consequence the company became the

Left: Founder George Lodge (right) and staff outside Lodge Tyre's' first premises in Rea Street, 1936.
Above: George Lodge pictured at the company's new premises in Bloomsbury Street, 1946. Right: Lodge Tyres Ashstead Row premises in the 1950s.

very first in Europe to be awarded ECE Regulation 109 approval - and as result of being the first Lodge proudly displays the certification number 000001 on its tyres.

Today the company employs more than 100 people and enjoys custom from some of the region's most prestigious fleets. Aptly the company logo is an elephant, an animal that never forgets - and the Lodge Tyre Co Ltd aims to ensure that it never forgets its customers.

As for the future, expansion remains the order of the day. To that end the company's commercial strategy is to concentrate on regional fleet operators, offering them a complete tyre management system normally enjoyed only by much larger fleets.

But however large the company becomes it will still remain a family business, taking genuine pride in being a Midlands concern.

Wood? you better believe it

When Edwin William Tinegate passed away at his home on Oakfield Road Selly Park in 1953 at the age of 82 he left behind him a name which would still be familiar to Birmingham folk more than half a century later.

The firm he founded, EW Tinegate Ltd timber merchants, is still to be found at 94 Lodge Road Birmingham today.

Though we may live in the plastic age happily wood, that most natural of materials, is still it seems as popular as ever. It's strange how evocative wood can be: the smell of fresh sawdust immediately conjures up all kinds of images - woodwork lessons at school, lucky dips at church Fayres and butchers shops back in the days when it was still usual for them to cover their floors with sawdust to soak up the blood.

But though you don't find much sawdust on floors these days you do find lots of wood everywhere you look. Despite the advantages of plastic natural wood still has a trick or two up its sylvan sleeve. It's strong, enduring and, goodness, doesn't it look so much better?

What's more wood will still be around when plastic, made from oil, has become just a memory.

Top left: *Edwin William Tinegate.*
Below: *An early 20th century photograph of E W Tinegate's Lodge Road Saw Mills.*

EW Tinegate is awaiting the day! It's already been around a very long time. A native of Hull, Edwin Tinegate founded the business in 1905; one of the main customers back then was the railways which bought sleepers from the firm. Twenty years later he had 17 men working for him in Birmingham as well as at the Littlemore saw mill three miles from Oxford.

The Littlemore steam driven saw mill would be sold in 1925 as the British economy began to stumble into the recession which would last until 1939.

The outbreak of war brought new demand for timber. It also brought huge risks, since the threat of fire, always a danger in timber yards, was now magnified enormously. Furthermore any 'normal' outbreak of fire might attract senemy bombers. Wood that had been regularly stored on the railway embankment was now moved in case sparks from passing locomotives ignited it.

Edwin's three sons, Eric, Harold and Kenneth, would eventually join him in the timber trade. Eric became Managing Director after his father's death, though only after spending some time as a prisoner of war in the Far East during the second world war. Kenneth, a member of Edgbaston Rowing Club, would compete in the first post war Olympic games rowing in the sculls.

Eric's two sons Peter and David would follow their father in joining the business, however after a short time with the company in the 1970s and 1980s other commitments would cause David to relocate to Devon.

Post war much would change in the business, not least the switch from steam which had until then driven the firm's lathes, saws and drills by belts. Also passing into history would be the stables which had once housed the firm's horses.

Today five full time staff using far more sophisticated machinery than in the past work for the company. The firm supplies DIY stores, renovators and specialists as well as factories in Birmingham and other timber merchants.

Meanwhile the answer to a question many of us have wondered about. Is wood today as good as it was? As many of us have suspected the quality of timber really has gone down over the decades, not least since much timber is forced to grow rather than maturing naturally over many decades.

The closely grained natural wood of first cut timber from virgin forrests, still familiar a generation or two ago, is now history. Wood today is taken from commercially run forests which have been planted, harvested, replanted and harvested yet again.

On the upside however, though the timber may not be of quite such fine quality as that available in years gone by we can take consolation in the knowledge that it is at least being bought from environmentally friendly sources and obtained from sustainable supplies.

The area around the timber yard is being redeveloped for housing, and it is surely only a matter of time before EW Tinegate Ltd faces moving to new premises. In the meantime the yard which supplied our fathers and grandfathers with timber is still located exactly where its founder left it, the evocative scent of fresh cut wood still perfuming the air around it, and managed today by Eric's son Peter Tinegate.

Above: An early Tinegate moulding machine.
Below: Eric Tinegate, circa 1970s.

Building the future

There are builders merchants and then there is THE builders merchant as EH Smith Ltd based in Sherbourne Road, Acocks Green is proud to describe itself as.

Today the company operates from no fewer than nine building materials centres located at Cannock, Chelmsford, Hemel Hempstead, Leicester, Peterborough, Shirley, Stourbridge, Olton and Witham. A further centre will be opened early 2005 in Sutton Coldfield.

The company is now one of Britain's largest independent builders merchants, but its start in the early 1920s was far more modest.

On 18th November 1922 a hardworking young entrepreneur, Howard Smith, set himself up as a very small builders merchant. His wife took care of administration at their Birmingham base whilst Howard delivered the goods personally, initially by motorcycle.

After many long hours and a great deal of hard work Howard Smith established his first real depot in Small Heath. Materials arrived by rail and were distributed, in rather larger volume than before, by horse and cart.

Within ten years the company had diversified into roofing, specialising in slating and

Top: Mr & Mrs EH Smith
Right: Bristol Cinema built with 12" Ibstock hand-made bricks supplied by EH Smith (Westhaven) Ltd in 1937.
Above right: A EH Smith farm building which was exhibited all over the country, circa 1950s.

tiling, forming a separate operation to deal with that aspect of the business.

But it was not all plain sailing. The Wall Street crash of 1929 saw EH Smith hit by bad debts of over a thousand pounds, a vast sum for the times.

Despite the inevitable difficulties of the 1930s the business continued to struggle forward and even expand.

The war years would see the company working hard to repair bomb damage. In November 1941 Howard Smith went to Coventry to supervise the 300 roofers taken out of the armed forces to re-roof the city. Fortunately the bombs which had landed in the Smiths Coventry depot, which had opened in 1936, had bounced across the yard

Smith's did the only sensible thing and bought the brickworks in order to ensure supply. Smiths were already in brick making having acquired Northcot Brick Ltd at Blockley in Gloucestershire ten years earlier.

Since then what would become the EH Smith group of companies would supply millions of bricks to discerning clients: in 1982 the company would supply the bricks for the Chapter House at St Albans opened by Her Majesty the Queen. The work at the St Albans Abbey Chapter House would subsequently earn the company the Quality Brickwork of the Year Award.

Expansion would continue throughout the 1990s with the Cannock depot opening in 1992 and Stourbridge in 1995. The following year all the builders merchants companies in the Group were merged into a single company EH Smith (Builders Merchants) Ltd, a move followed almost immediately by the acquisition of the Mid Essex Trading Company based in Chelmsford.

In the year ending 31st December 1923 the business made a net profit of just £67 and 16 shillings.

Founder Howard Smith would surely have been astonished, and disbelieving, if anyone had suggested to him that in the future his motorbike would be replaced by a whole fleet of trucks, and that in the opening decade of the new millennium his business would have an annual turnover of a remarkable £75 million.

without exploding; bravely if perhaps unwisely, young Ken Smith, today the company Chairman, had actually carried one of the bombs out of the depot.
In London 50 EH Smith operatives, there to repair flying bomb damage, had a miraculous escape when a massive German V2 rocket landed where they had been working in Deptford, just two hours after they had left for their monthly break.

In the 1950s more large government contracts began to appear. The company was engaged to distribute farm buildings made from recycled Anderson bomb shelters. The company now also began providing civil engineering materials for motorway building, notably the M1, though the company was also involved in the very first stretch of British motorway, the Preston by-pass section of the M6 in Lancashire. When the first stretch of the M1 opened in 1959, the year in which company founder Howard Smith passed away, all its drainage had been supplied by his company.

The following years would be ones of diversification, expansion and acquisitions.

Brick making would be one of those areas of growth. In 1960 Smith's had been supplying specialist bricks for the Stevenage Police Station, which were being sourced from the small Bovingdon Brickworks. When the brickworks announced it was to close half way through the contract

Top left: EH Smith (Westhaven) Ltd's Shirley depot, circa 1950. Above left: The Chairman and Directors pictured in 1982 the year of the company's 60th Anniversary. Below: An EH Smith new style truck, 2004.

Vision for the Future

Few family owned companies can survive decades of change and strong competition and yet still remain profitable, but Scrivens Ltd, the Optical and Hearing Care specialists is a local success story.

Scrivens, established by Solomon ('Sol') Scriven in the heart of Birmingham, is today the UK's largest combined Optical and Hearing Retailer, and is currently run by the third generation of the Scrivens family.

Sol Scriven married Milly Lewis in Glasgow in August 1929; their children, Dorothy ('Dodo') and Harvey, both were involved in the business. Dodo met Alexander ('Sasha') Georgevic as a student at Birmingham University and they married in July 1960. Sasha then joined the business, later becoming Chairman when Solomon died in 1979. Today, Dodo and Sasha's two sons, Nicholas (Chairman and Managing Director) and Mark (Legal and Property Director), drive the Company forward, still upholding the same high level of quality and professionalism that has become ingrained in the Company for over sixty years.

Sol Scriven was born in Leeds on 13th December 1900. A qualified pharmacist, he was also an astute businessman. Spotting an opportunity in optics, he opened his first branch in Ward End in 1938 with his brother Maurice, a qualified optician. Sol then qualified as an optician himself and they built the business up steadily together.

Scrivens' business grew rapidly in the West Midlands after the Second World War. Anticipating changes within the optical industry, Sol had already opened a number of additional branches ready for when the NHS first introduced free sight tests in 1948. This crucial expansion paid off; as the branches saw customers

literally 'queuing round the block' for their free sight tests. This success prompted the first 'Prescription House' to be opened to manufacture spectacles. This had very modest beginnings, situated in Hockley above a stable. It is said that the smell of straw and horses would actually reach into the rooms above! The first Head Office was situated above a branch in Paradise Street and was run by Sol with the help of just a book keeper and a secretary. With expansion, both Prescription House and Head Office have moved throughout the years and are located today in Halesowen and Central Birmingham respectively.

Always business-minded, Sol was keen to continue the Company's growth, but an early experience with a lending bank would change the Company's attitude towards investment forever. On arranging a business loan, he felt so badly treated that he swore never to borrow money again. To this day, Scrivens has expanded only by reinvesting its own funds to stay free of debt and remain financially strong.

The launch of Hearing Care in the late fifties heralded a whole new era at Scrivens, broadening the Company into a new marketplace. At this time, there was no legislation for dispensing within the hearing industry. However, under the direction of Sasha Georgevic, Scrivens applied the practices it had developed within the optical division in order to perpetuate the same high standards of quality and service. In this, Scrivens set the standard for the industry, as many of the principles introduced were carried forward into national legislation through guidelines introduced by the Hearing Aid Council ten years later.

Political and professional involvement in the industry has always been a key element of Scrivens' outlook and the business has benefited from ongoing involvement with governing bodies, including the General Optical Council, the British Optical Association and the Hearing Aid Council. This ongoing commitment to the industry has helped the Company to cultivate an enviable position in the marketplace.

Most impressively, Sasha Georgevic was a member of the inaugural Hearing Aid Council in 1968 and his input shaped the legislative framework that still regulates the industry today.

Top: Founder, Solomon 'Sol' Scriven.
Above: Early spectacles and eye glasses.

The Company has come a long way from its modest beginnings. There are now over 100 optical and hearing care branches plus over 400 hundred hearing sites in partner outlets nation-wide. Scrivens employs nearly 1,000 staff throughout the Group.

Under the current leadership, expansion has continued apace in recent years. The acquisition of Leadbeater and Peters added 18 Northern based branches in the 1980s and the purchase of Robert Hutchinson Opticians in 1991 added a further eight branches in East Anglia. The most significant acquisition was of 40 Melson Wingate branches, based predominantly in the South, in July 2002. In the last year, Scrivens has added branches in Rugby, Rushden, Eastbourne, Southsea, Aylesbury, Hove, Dover and Crowborough.

Scrivens' directors have collectively spent twenty two years sitting on the Hearing Aid Council with each member having been asked to sit for the maximum two consecutive terms. Indeed Mark Georgevic is a current member of the Hearing Aid Council.

Over the years, Scrivens has evolved in response to the changes in the optical and hearing industries. In particular, when the NHS ceased to provide free spectacles in the 1970s and abolished free sight tests in the 1990s, Scrivens adapted its position to compete in the new 'retail' marketplace. It took advantage of developments in the contact lens market to offer an extensive range and professional service as well as pioneering regular contact lens schemes through the launch of its own highly successful Contact Lens regular replacement and aftercare scheme Lensplan.

Equally, as legislation changed within the hearing industry, Scrivens Hearing also adapted. In the 1980s the business moved from dispensing hearing aids in the home to trading from its own optical retail outlets. Hundreds of further hearing care sites were added through partnerships with other opticians and health centres.

Scrivens has always been at the forefront of developments in optical and hearing care products. Today's spectacles are a far cry from the NHS glasses of the early years. Using materials such as titanium, modern frames are light and durable; while lenses are thinner and lighter making 'milk-bottle' glasses a thing of the past. Contact lenses today offer superb vision with excellent comfort and convenience, catering for a wider range of visual requirements than ever before, while hearing aids have embraced digital technology and can even be virtually invisible in use. Product development has always been accompanied by intensive staff training, so that customers can always expect professional advice and care based on their own individual needs.

There are many factors that have contributed to Scrivens' success over the years, but the enduring element is the ability of all those within the business, from senior management to the most recent and junior staff to be 'ever flexible' to meet new opportunities, or challenges in the marketplace. As a result, Scrivens has remained a strong family owned company and is today the UK's biggest optical and hearing care retailer with branches across the country. Each successive generation has built upon the reputation and success achieved in the early years and has retained a professional commitment to putting the customer first and, hopefully, improving the quality of people's lives from an optical and hearing perspective.

Top: *A Scrivens branch based in Wolverhampton in the 1960s.* *Below:* *One of Scrivens Optical and Hearing Care branches, 2004.*

Acknowledgments

The publishers would like to thank

Birmingham Library Services

Women's Royal Voluntary Services - South West Division

Andrew Mitchell

Steve Ainsworth